Straight Talk
about
Window Cleaning
Bidding

Straight Talk about Window Cleaning Bidding

By John Baxter

CRYSTAL PRESS   SIMI VALLEY

The text in this book is composed of CaslonOldFace
Hv BT 11/13.2 with displays set in CaslonOldFace Hv
BT petite caps.
Printed in the United States of America

ISBN 0-9632123-2-X

Library of Congress Cataloging in Publication Data
Baxter, John M.
Straight Talk about Window Cleaning Bidding
By John Baxter

10 9 8 7 6 5 4 3
Copyright © 2003 John Baxter

Crystal Press
Simi Valley, CA

To Marty Racenstein

A young book collector perusing the shelves of his mentor's used bookstore spied a volume of Ulysses by James Joyce.

He tugged on the book till it fell free of the other books on the shelf.

Holding it up for the owner to view he asked, "How much is this book worth?"

The old man glanced up from his own book and peered over his spectacles for a moment then returned to his book and sighed, "Whatever someone is willing to pay for it, my young friend."

Table of Contents

Introduction

This book is a long time in coming. It began years ago as short articles for the American Window Cleaner Magazine. Window cleaners asked me many questions about the bidding process, and I promised myself that someday I would write a book about bidding.

Well, that day has arrived.

Starting into the window cleaning business, I remembered how hard it was to gather information about the business. When I started 20 years ago, a young man with enthusiasm for the business but not much knowledge, I stopped and spoke with every window cleaner I could find. I gathered much knowledge and information about the business. Sadly, most window cleaners looked upon me as a threat. Few window cleaners would talk about window cleaning techniques never mind the bidding process. A few were polite but many were down right rude.

Luckily, though, I found a few window cleaners that did not view me as a threat but as another human being trying to earn a living.

Like the proverbial "Good Samaritan," each offered suggestions, helped me learn, and empowered me with a spirit that I could succeed in the window cleaning business.

I never forgot these people. They are as fresh in my mind today as they were 25-years ago, and I am forever thankful for their help and friendship.

Today's beginning window cleaners do not have to learn the business by themselves. An organization exists to help them get started. It's called the International Window Cleaning Association.

Within the IWCA are the most generous and knowledgeable professionals in the industry. At the IWCA, cleaning professionals can receive answers to any question related to the window cleaning industry because of the vast and comprehensive networking system.

No one should be an island in business. The more you involve yourself in the IWCA the more knowledgeable you become. Your peers and associates from around the world will challenge you to the highest levels of professional-ism.

I wrote this book with the beginner in mind. As I typed, I imagined such a person next to me with all the eagerness for the business that I once had.

I wanted to share everything I learned from my experience and the experience of others in a hope that window cleaners would learn how to earn enough money to create the safest and most professional window cleaning enterprise possible.

I also wanted the book to be easy to use and simple to read. I recommend reading the book straight through to the end; you will find many suggestions and tips. However, if time is important, you can pick and choose whatever chapters you need.

The information is divided into blocks of subjects that can be started at any chapter.

You can skip around to different chapters to find whatever you need now. Or, skip the reading material and get to the information quickly for basic bidding questions. I placed a summary of the most important information about bidding in the appendix.

My hope for you and all window cleaners can be summed up in a story told to me by a young couple who owned a window cleaning business near San Francisco.

Each year this husband and wife window

cleaning team, takes a major vacation to some exotic spot in the world. Their trip to the airport is done ceremoniously, the same way each time. They hire a limousine to take them to the airport and while on the way, they open a bottle of champagne and pour two glasses. They raise their glasses to each other and say, "Here's to dirty windows," then they "clink" glasses and savor their success.

May all window cleaners feel that success knowing they earned enough money to do what they want to do, when they want to do it. All this is possible for window cleaners who learn to bid properly.

Now, it's time to begin.

I wish you well.

John Baxter

BIDDING THEORY, QUESTIONS, AND PHILOSOPHY

...Not all in that order

Chapter One

BASIC BIDDING

Correct window cleaning bidding will make the difference between building a successful window cleaning enterprise and going out of business. It will mean the difference between whether a person can vacation in Hawaii with the entire family or need to work seven days a week. It will mean the difference between hiring and keeping good employees and training them completely and safely or hiring and losing employees constantly because the owner can't pay them enough to keep them happy, nor can he or she train them properly because not enough money exists for proper training.

So much time is spent worrying about how

15

to clean a window properly that we sometimes lose sight of ultimately why we're washing the window: to make money. There's nothing wrong with making money, even a lot of money.

The question is "How much is 'a lot' of money?" For each person the answer will be different based upon one's comfort level with money. If you were earning $9 an hour on your last job, you might feel a bit uncomfortable earning $100 an hour or more for a job. You may feel as though you are cheating the customer. Where another window cleaner knows with today's living expenses that $100 an hour is profitable and necessary for his style of living. What does the customer think? That will vary, too.

True story, an experienced, 20-year, veteran of the window cleaning industry left one morning to bid two major window cleaning jobs. The first job was located 25 miles south of his home. The property manager called him out to bid on the exterior window cleaning of five large, two-story office buildings with one row of windows wrapped around each floor for each building. After inspecting all the buildings, checking for calcium deposits, deciding the manpower needed, the time involved, and the equipment needed, he wrote up the bid and presented it to the property manager who promptly looked at the bid and declared, "Oh, that's way too high; I can't pay that price."

The window cleaner said he would review the bid when he went back to his office and see if he could "sharpen his pencil" just a bit.

Next, the window cleaner traveled about 10 miles north of the job he just bid and met with another property manager. This property manager also wanted a bid on the exterior window cleaning of her buildings. What struck the window cleaner immediately was the similarity of the industrial park he just bid and the one he was about to bid. Both parks' buildings were almost identical; in fact, it was possible that both parks were developed by the same builder. The only major difference was that the first park had rough, sand blasted walls and the other park had smooth white walls. The glass looked the same: two ribbons of glass wrapped around each building. Again, the window cleaner hiked around each building inspecting all the plates, same process as the first industrial park. When he finished calculating the bid, which was the exact same price given to the first property manager, he handed the bid to the second property manager who glanced at the bid and promptly said, "How can you do the job that cheaply?"

The moral of the story: Everyone has their price; it just varies from person-to-person.

Potential customers will have many opinions and views about how much to pay for window cleaning. As a window cleaner soliciting potential customers, it's easy to get caught up in the conversations and try to get the job at all costs.

After all, one of the objectives in business is to increase sales which, in turn, hopefully means an increase in profits. However, the two goals may not go hand-and-hand. It's entirely possible, if a window cleaner is not careful, to gain large amounts of business and actually lose money.

Window cleaners want to earn a fair price for their services, yet at the same time customers want value for their dollar and to keep their expenses at a minimum. The two forces collide and somewhere within the variables affecting today's window cleaning market a fair price is found.

You know that feeling of success or will soon know it. That feeling knowing that you did a professional job for a price that is satisfying.

When working on the job site, the window cleaner knows after a while whether or not his price is good for the window work being done. If the window cleaner bid the job correctly, the price agreed upon is within the ballpark of profit, then the job feels much easier to complete. The window cleaner should be able to complete the job without having to rush through the work.

If, on the other hand, the window cleaner underbid the job, a depressing feeling can creep into one's mind knowing that the hourly or daily rate for service set by the window cleaner did not get met. Nothing, nothing can be as frustrating or depressing as working at a job site knowing the price is under — sometimes way under — what one expected to make per hour or per day for window cleaning services.

That's when window cleaners rush;
that's when accidents happen;
that's when quality and professionalism go out the proverbial window.

Sometimes a window cleaner thinks the

price for window cleaning services is within an adaquate estimate for work completed only to find out later he or she did not consider paying Uncle Sam and when tax season rolls around, their bank account is woefully inadequate to pay out money for taxes or maybe insurance.

Hopefully, the lesson will help the window cleaner rethink the pricing strategy and overcome the fear of asking for a raise or charging new customers the newer rates. The fear of losing customers or not getting the job because another company came in and underbid you is a real fear, but so is the fear of not being able to pay your expenses.

Window cleaning is a great business, yet it can become a nightmare if the owner consistently underbids the work, but, if bid properly, window cleaning can be everything one expects from job satisfaction to high income.

"If you don't know where you are going, you will wind up somewhere else."

The Wise Window Cleaner

Chapter Two

TEN QUESTIONS FOR THE BEGINNER

(If you are an experienced window cleaner, then move on to the next chaper)

Setting up a business with a specific business plan to be attained within a certain period of time helps an aspiring window cleaning entreprenuer to attain success in building a viable business. Like the builder of a house who designs how the structure will be built, so too the beginning business person should set down how the business will be built before the business starts to grow and prosper.

Before you begin, though, some questions need answers. These questions need a little soul searching, and your honesty will make the difference between enjoying the business while earning a good living or hating your life.

1. Do you really like the business?

There's an old saying: "Do what you love and the money will follow." If you've entered this business and you find the work just okay or even slightly boring, then do one of two things: Either try other types of window cleaning (i.e. try cleaning storefront windows if you have only cleaned house windows or visa versa) or try other related services like steam cleaning.

Or, take the role of manager and hire others to clean the windows.

The alternative? Do yourself a favor and get out of the business. If it's not something you like, why punish yourself? Find another type of business. This doesn't mean that even if you hate the window cleaning business that you can't be successful at window cleaning. That's far from true. There are highly successful window cleaners that abhor the business yet stay in the business either because they don't know what else to do or because they inherited the business or because the money is so good — which it can be — that they don't want to get out of their financial comfort zone to transition into something to his or her liking. Yes, the money in the window cleaning business can be highly lucrative, but all the money in the world will not bring happiness if deep inside you dislike the business. Some window cleaners are wealthy but miserable.

There's a true story about a man who sat at a machine that made screws all day long. He worked at the machine with a smile, a peaceful look on his face. He had no bills to speak of and just took his paychecks and stuck them in the bank.

He had built up considerable wealth (millions of dollars) when his coworkers began urging him to get out of the business and go enjoy life. He always said that he does enjoy life; he loves his work. Later that year he gave a million dollars to a charity.

Do you enjoy the business enough that you would clean windows for free? One window cleaner enjoyed the business so much that he went around to his friend's homes at Christmas time and cleaned his friend's windows for free as his gift to them.

Maybe you like the business but you feel you need an "attitude adjustment." Then check out World Famous Pike Place Fish Market and watch people enjoying their work in action. The workers at this Seattle fish market are famous for their incredibly positive on-the-job attitude.

Imagine the way most fish markets sell seafood. You order three pounds of salmon and a worker tosses some fillet on the scale and says, "Anything else," with a dull voice that says this job is dull and boring.

Now look at the way **Pike Place Fish Market** sells that same salmon. A worker yells out with enthusiasm, "One salmon on the way!" Another worker yells back, "One salmon." Suddenly a five-pound silver salmon is flying 20 feet through the air and caught in the pink fish-wrap. Some-one else shouts "crab!" and suddenly you see crabs flying through the air. Sometimes they catch them, sometimes they don't. Occasionally, the workers grab the customer and make her catch the incoming fish. The humorous com-ments, camaraderie and banter have the custom-ers laughing and enjoying the fun atmosphere.

The Pike Place Market workers have taken what could be a routine, mundane job and, with an attitude adjustment, made the job and busi-ness more fun for themselves and ultimately their customers. Workers enjoy coming to work, cus-tomers love to come shop. The fish market is so famous that many times crowds of onlookers come just to watch the show, and it is a show.

If you can't get to Seattle, then check-out the book Fish written by Stephen Lundin, John Christensen, and Harry Paul. The story is about Pike Place workers and their four principles to a better work attitude: "Play," "Make Their Day," "Be There," and "Choose Your Attitude."

Okay, so you've decided that window cleaning is a business for you, that you have bad days but overall you enjoy the business. Next question.

competition stiff where little or no work can be acquired and what work you find seems too low in price? If the window cleaning market gives you any room for entry, then ...

6. Who is the competition?

You found an area you like and you know what type of window cleaning you want to target—i.e. house windows. Who is your competition? How will you compete for the window cleaning in your area? How will your service be different from your competitors? In any business, it's important to know who else is offering a similar service. Hopefully, your attitude toward your competitors is professional maybe even friendly for two reasons: First, most regions have room for another window cleaner, so why raise your blood pressure over a few dollars? As a window cleaner once told me, "In a hundred years, no one will care or even remember who cleaned the windows on a building, but the memory of how one was treated by another human being lingers for a lifetime." How do you wish to be remembered? Second, one of the fastest ways to build a window cleaning business is to buy out your competitors. If you are not on speaking terms with your competitors, how are you going to buy their business? Know your competition and act professionally.

7. How will your company be different?

One new company owner attempting to enter the storefront window cleaning business in his town found that the competition cleaned windows on a weekly basis and only weekly. He decided to market his service by offering twice a month or once a month service. He could provide a service at a slightly lower rate but not that much lower since the competitors kept weekly window cleaning prices low to keep out other window cleaners. By offering twice a month service, this new window cleaner was able to fill a niche in the window cleaning market in his area because some customers only wanted twice a month or once a month service. This strategy gained him a foothold in the market, and he was later able to expand to other cities.

The same thing happened when he decided to venture into window cleaning of mid-rise office buildings. In this case, he approached the window cleaning from a water-fed pole standpoint. He decided that if he needed a ladder for a job, he would not bid the job. This method served him well, and he was able to slowly develop an efficient mid-rise window cleaning service that avoided, for the most part, the use of ladders on the job. Many of his competitors used ladders and lots of labor to clean the same type of mid-rise buildings. He marketed his service toward only these types of buildings and avoided the jobs requiring a ladder. Another cleaner in a related business felt the same way. This janitorial company only selected buildings with at least 90% carpet and little or no floor tile. The

reason for this was he felt that tile was a difficult and time consuming to cleaning.

8. How much do you want to earn per hour? per day?

Just earning money washing windows does
not mean you can earn a living unless you know
your hourly rate is high enough to cover your
expenses and pay you a good salary. As of this
printing, most window cleaners would like to
earn between $50 and $100 per hour. Not that
they always earn that, but that is a goal.

9. What goals do you want to accomplish in your first year?

Be specific. Write down all the things you
want to accomplish and then set about to make
them happen. Maybe you want to target a certain monthly sales goal. Maybe you want to just
manage employees. Some window cleaners po-
sition themselves as a manager and never as a
window cleaner. What do you want to accomplish?

10. Now, get started. What goals do you want to complete by the end of this week?

Write down what you want to accomplish
now. In fact, every week write down the equipment you need to buy, the number of sales calls
you want to make, the business activities you
want to accomplish, whatever will help you attain your goals for your business.

All these questions and more play an important role in developing your mentality toward the bidding process.

"The customer receiving the best price will also be the customer that complains the most."

The Wise Window Cleaner

Chapter 3

STRATEGIES TO PRICING

Customers more than anything else want value for their hard-earned money. That's why customers decide to accept a certain price; the customer feels the services they will receive are a good value for their money.

What's interesting, though, is each customer's perception of value for their money. No two customers look at the value of a window cleaning service in the same way, and in some cases their expectation about the window cleaning costs will tell the bidder much about the potential customer.

So, how does a window cleaner choose the best price, the one that will bring in the highest profit and still offer enough value so the customer remains happy with the service?

Window cleaning companies approach bidding strategies in various ways; however, all or most of these bidding strategies can be broken down into four categories: Top of Market, Upmarket, Competitive Pricing, Bottom End. Each bidding category, strategy, or philosphy offers the window cleaner different options in different cleaning situations. Even though window cleaning companies tend to stick to one style of bidding, each category can be used in different window cleaning situations.

Top of Market

Achieve the most profit possible, set prices well above the industry average for that area and expect a possible short term relationship, these are the characteristics of the Top of Market strategy. The bid is set to the maximum price an owner deems conceivable for the window cleaning in the area. The bidder may use this strategy for several reasons:

First, the company may be the only company in the area that can complete the job. With few or no competitors, the price for services is free to float to the level that the free enteprise market will bear.

Given the lack of competition, companies that take advantage of the situation generate high profits in the short term. Generally, though, the free market system has a way of balancing itself. One company reaping large profits in one segment of the market will eventually feel the bite of competition. The old adage, "Excess profits brings ruinous competition," applies to this strategy.

Companies trying to hold on to their market share with this pricing strategy should either provide the highest quality service or expect to offer some discounting of the price, maybe even some deep discounting (which is not recommended) if they expect to hold on to their market share.

Second, the company may estimate a high degree of difficulty in completing the job, so the bidder sets the price high enough to cover any unforeseen costs in completing the job like extra time that may be needed or to include a risk factor to the job.

Third, the company believes strongly in providing Top of Market service, quality unsurpassed in their city, town or state. Their window cleaning service represents the best that money can buy and that establishes who they are as a window cleaning firm. When these companies clean windows, the service provided carries with it a professionalism displayed in many areas in the company's way of doing business.

Sometimes the customer is willing to pay more not for the window cleaning but the security or peace-of-mind the company has established within the market. One example of this is a maintenance company whose owner, Gary, is a police officer. All Gary's customers know he is a police officer in the community. Hiring a company whose owner is a police officer gives these customers a sense of security, a feeling that by allowing Gary and his employees access to the buildings both inside and out, they feel safer; they worry less about possessions, materials, products or anything of value being lifted from

33

the premises. These customers are willing to pay a higher price for the security and Gary knows this. He sells the security angle to new customers and reminds his current customers that they can feel at peace knowing he and his workers are on the job. Some of his customers past and present include large pharmaceutical companies, stereo equipment dealers, and high end recreational equipment manufacturers, customers with a need for high security on the premises.

Does Gary's company feel the pinch of lower price competition? Absolutely. Gary's pricing can be two to four times higher than his competition. Almost daily competitors attempt to convince Gary's customers to switch services. As long as Gary maintains the paragon image his customers expect, Gary, for the most part, keeps his customers. The responsibility to maintain the highest, the ultimate in professional quality, rests on Gary. When that image slips is when Gary loses his customers. On one occasion, Gary lost a substantial account to a company that bid half the price Gary charged the company. After some investigation as to why he lost the account, Gary uncovered a weakness within his company. The high, professional quality work that his client expected day in and day out from Gary had fallen, and the company decided that value for their money was not what they expected.

Yes, the security in knowing a police officer managed the work was there, but the quality of work (especially from one employee) had fallen off. So, the company decided to make a change. Gary realized if he is to keep his customers, he must continue to provide the highest quality service and, in Gary's case, a sense of security to his customers.

A similar company based in the midwest likewise focused on being in the Top of Market in terms of price and service. For many, many years now, Terry, the owner of this six-person, high-rise window cleaning company, has dominated the high rise window cleaning in his city. What sets Terry's company apart from the competition is, again, the highest quality service with no short-cuts taken in cleaning, the strictest adherence to safety standards, and comprehensive knowledge of high-rise window cleaning situations. For this service Terry commands the highest price service, in some cases twice as much as his competition, and Terry also dominates the market sector with eighty percent of the high-rise work in the town.

Does Terry feel the sting of competition? Absolutely. Terry loses work to competitors and almost as quickly acquires the work back when, in a few years or less, the old customer realizes the quality of work was not what Terry provided, or the other company used risky window cleaning methods to clean the high-rise buildings, or the other company's employees were not professional in appearance or manner. Customers, like Terry's, want value for their money.

This high-end service oriented company policy works best in two particular target markets in the window cleaning business: homes and office complexes which includes low, medium, and high rise buildings. Many homeowners want the surety of knowing they and their possessions are safe and whatever work is done in the highest professional manner.

The Top of the Market strategy will be most successful in soft areas of a window cleaner's target market and in areas where customers have money. That sounds simplistic but still needs to be said. These high-end customers are usually found in the upper end of the market: office buildings, estate houses or large homes. This does not mean the customers with office buildings and estates do not challenge a window cleaner's price. In some cases the rich have their money because of their miserly habits; they are the proverbial Mr. Scrooge. But, as mentioned, it's the customers with money and willing to spend the money that makeup the majority of "Top of the Market" customers. Generally, the people with money are in this target market bracket.

The other area where Top of the Market works is in the soft areas of the market or areas where no window cleaner has solicited customers for work or an area where a window cleaner has stopped cleaning windows or the window cleaner is so bad that customers can't wait to have another window cleaning service. All three of these scenarios are possible and by probing around different areas of the storefront window cleaning market, a window cleaner can acquire a "feel" or "a pulse" on the storefront window cleaning in his or her community. That's important for the long run survival of any business: to know what is happening in the industry.

Window cleaners that target storefront windows for their business face a few problems when attempting to use the Top of the Market system.

Storefront window cleaning is one of the easiest ways to start a window cleaning business. Thus, the competition stiffens due to many entry level, new window cleaners soliciting window cleaning work. Of course, a new window cleaner's prices will vary, but generally, the method used by many neophyte window cleaners will be cheap pricing. In some sections of some cities around the country, new window cleaners will walk into other window cleaner's storefront accounts an average of once a month — or more —trying to pick up new business. Sometimes the competition is from cutthroat competitors, sometimes the threat comes from new window cleaners just trying to break into the business, get a foothold in an industry they are now learning.

The way many established storefront window cleaning companies stay competitive is by keeping the price of the service competitive and cleaning windows in volume.

What new-to-the-business window cleaners haven't learned yet is that trying to build a business by taking another window cleaner's jobs is a tough way to build a professional, high-quality business, and that in the long run, these window cleaners must cut corners: only clean the lower half of the window (called "haircutting" the job) or only clean some of the windows (called "rounding out the building").

Sadly, at the end of the year, the window cleaner doesn't have enough money to pay taxes or insurance or some other major expense like vehicle expenses (the car wears out and money must be set aside to buy another means of transportation eventually.) These window cleaners did not think ahead to the hidden costs of doing business; they usually don't last five years; they burn out from cleaning too many windows at too cheap a price, or they just can't pay their bills with what they earn.

An example of this is the story of one new cleaner in Southern California who announced to his peers in the cleaning business that he was picking up work at an astounding rate. When others in the business asked how he managed to grow his business so quickly, he told them it was easy. He just offered his work at half the competitor's prices and planned on making his money on "volume work." Within a few months this new cleaner had enough work to hire two people. He bought a brand new van for his workers and for the next year, the bright blue van with the magnetic signs on the doors could be seen zipping around town going to the new accounts.

After a year, though, the van disappeared along with the new cleaner and his company. Other cleaners stepped in and picked up his work at twice the price (remember soft market). The new window cleaners inquired as to what happened to the other cleaner. All the old customers knew was that he was no longer in business, that he had moved out of the area, and that the Internal Revenue Service wanted to talk.

This story represents what can happen when you do not watch your pricing structure, or you fear the possiblity of overcharging your customers. With Top of the Market pricing strategy remember the key to this pricing is finding customers with money willing to pay for a perceived value for their money. People willing to pay can be found in many types of markets.

The other factors that affect Top of the Market strategy would be competition and the economy. Attempting to set higher prices works best in a growing, expanding market where the demand is strong and where there is money. Trying to set prices higher in a shrinking or falling or low economy is like trying to swim up river. It's tough to create that type of business.

Upmarket
This strategy, in a market where the demand is strong and the market growing, a window cleaner is free to move the bid higher. In this market strategy, the window cleaner sets prices above the average to obtain a reasonable volume but has the flexibility built into the pricing to lower the price slightly if necessary.

Window cleaners that set the price higher than the majority of the competition, send a psychological message that their service offers higher value than the competition.

A study completed years ago compared two dust cleaning products sold at the grocery stores around the country. Both products, manufactured by different companies, stood on the shelf next to each other, both products worked the same way. The only real differences in the physical appearance of the two was the product wrapping and the price. One product was priced 12 percent higher in price, enough of a price difference that the variance put the products in different categories in the eyes of the consumers, otherwise the products looked identical.

In this study, customers were asked to rank the two products. Invariably, the customers ranked the higher priced product a better product. The rationale used by most people was that the slightly higher price must mean that the product is of better quality. In this particular study, the higher priced dust cleaner outsold the other product. Why? Because customers wanted the product that they thought would be the better product based on the higher price.

Dusting products and window cleaning represent two different types of cleaning, but this pricing psychology may work for some window cleaners in certain areas of the country and in certain types of target markets.

One window cleaner, Mario, in Southern California decided to price his product just above his competition, but he also made sure he offered his customers the best service. For years he traveled in his town and neighboring communities with a crew of four. He knew, and his customers knew, he cost a bit more than the competition, but he produced quality work. Not only that, but with the prices he charged he could take that little extra time and offer a professionalism that the competition could not because of their low price. He, also, provided uniforms, paid worker's compensation insurance, hired his workers as employees — yes, employees, not independent contractors. Hiring independent contractors is cheaper for the employer but can cause him or her major problems with the IRS or former employees. Mario didn't become rich, but he made a comfortable living for a number of years, and he could sleep at night.

Competitive Pricing

With competitive pricing, the bidder starts with the price he or she would like to receive for the window cleaning service and then works backward to the minimum cost of providing the service. The window cleaner is fully aware of the costs of running a business and the salary needed to survive in life. The way a window cleaner does that is by competitive pricing.

Competitive pricing is the type of pricing that happens in most areas of window cleaning competition today. Many window cleaning companies exist in a given market area and each has a comparable service. The storefront window cleaning business is a good example of competitive pricing.

In many communities two or more window cleaners compete for the storefront window cleaning. In some cases five to ten companies will drop off a card offering to clean one little store with two 4'by8' panes and a glass door. In this environment the competition for the job can be intense; the bidding price might drop with each window cleaner that enters the shop.

What's important is that the window cleaner knows "when to hold and when to fold."

By knowing what your time is worth and by knowing all your expenses right down to the income tax and social security payments, you'll be better prepared to learn to walk away from work not worth doing.

Case in point, there once was a window cleaner that serviced a business office complex of high-rise and low-rise office buildings that stretched two city blocks. This window cleaner and his crew retained this contract with the property manager year after year. Another window cleaner wished to get the contract but knew that the first window cleaner had the inside edge; he also knew that the other window cleaner and his crew would meet or beat any bid offered by competitors for the next year's window cleaning contract.

The new window cleaner, in order to test how far the original cleaner was willing to go, decided to cut the price by two-thirds the original bid or what he guessed was two-thirds. At this price window cleaner B knew that window cleaner A would lose money if he matched the bid. There was no way possible for window cleaner A to make a dime. The contract was worth about $100,000 a year in cleaning. Window cleaner B came in with a bid around $30,000 for the year. Well, window cleaner A sweat a little when he heard the other guy's bid, but true to his word he met B's bid and was awarded the contract. Window Cleaner B sat back and watched Window Cleaner A trying to provide a service that was below his costs. What happened? Window Cleaner A died of a heart attack.

This story is a slight exaggeration of the real thing, but brings home the point. Whether you are dealing with $20 jobs or $20,000 jobs, know your competitive limit and know when to say enough and walk away with a clean con-

science that you did your best, and that's all you
can do.

Many window cleaners believe that when
they lose a job, they sense a better paying job
will come their way. Many, many window cleaners have shared this scenario of losing out on
one job but another one falling into their laps,
or they lose a window cleaning contract that
spurs them on to find something even better.

Window cleaners with high end pricing
and those that seem to price their services at
the bottom end are not necessarily in different
cities, communities or different states. In many
cases both types of window cleaners live and
work in the same community. Each has decided
how to approach the business and set their goals
accordingly. To get their price, each window
cleaner may approach the market differently.

Bottom End

In some instances the window cleaner re-
duces the price for the service to below minimum wage just to get the job or keep the job.
You've heard the advertisements on television
that say: "Hey, we'll meet or beat any deal."
Businesses trying to survive in a highly competitive market will flex the pricing structure to acquire or keep business. (Many, many years ago a
window cleaner would offer his services for free
for one month, six months, even a year.)

Why would window cleaners offer such
drastic price cutting?

One reason for price cutting was to get a
foothold in a community or to establish their
business. Even today some window cleaners try

to lower their competitive prices way below even their costs in an attempt to increase their customer base.

In the short run, the strategy of cutting the other guy's price in half or worse just to get the job does get some clients — usually not the best clientele, but definitely some customers to work with. In the long run, however, this strategy can literally make a window cleaner hate life since the window cleaner isn't earning enough money per job to pay the bills and earn a living, or the strategy puts the window cleaner out of business or "six feet under."

A second reason that some window cleaners almost "gave window cleaning services away" was the fact that at one time years ago an established window cleaning business commanded great selling prices. A window cleaner back in the 1950's and 1960's and early 70's might be able to sell an established business for 10 to 20 times the monthly gross.

Imagine building an established window cleaning route with no other competition for blocks nor would another window cleaner enter into the area to solicit. Competitors respected each other's routes either out of fear of retaliation or respect for the owner, and the routes stayed together.

Once the route was established and respected as that window cleaner's route, the window cleaner could move prices up to a comfortable level. Occasionally, a new window cleaner may try to take a job in the route area and sometimes succeed. But a competitive window cleaner would meet the new person's price no matter what the price or beg and plead to get the job back.

Tales of a window cleaner on his knees literally crying, begging to get the job back actually happened. Once the window cleaner was able to get the job back or even if he wasn't able to, he found out the new competitor, and did his best to wreck the new guy's route usually by seeking out his work and trying to take his customers away.

The stories of window cleaner's inhumanity to other window cleaners actually gets much worse, but you get the idea. For the most part, though, this feudal system of territories is dead.

Yes, such routes and systems of agreements to respect each other's routes do exist to a certain extent today usually among the older generation of window cleaners, guys that used boarhair bristle brushes (replaced by the inexpensive stripwashers today) to scrub windows, and if you're not familiar with boarhair brushes or never used one, then count yourself in the new generation of window cleaners.

Once the competitive pressure has gone, then the window cleaner has some flexiblity to move prices higher.

The third reason for price cutting is to not let another window cleaner get a foothold in a particular center or complex. At one time window cleaners had a saying: "If another window cleaner gets a job in one shopping center then chances are good that the new window cleaner will be able to pick up two more jobs in that same center." The new window cleaner is able to establish that job and maybe a route.

It's easy to go around to the other stores in the shopping center trying to "steal" the work away from other window cleaners. If a window cleaner is established in that particular shopping center or, for that matter, an entire community, then it is worth the window cleaner's time, money, and effort to keep all other window cleaners out of the area. Usually, this price war mentality takes a toll on the new window cleaner who eventually gets discouraged (which can take a few years) and moves on either to another town, another form of the business such as houses or office buildings or another type of service such as carpet cleaning or steam cleaning or any combination. Sometimes the new window cleaner just hangs up the squeegee and goes into another business altogether different from the window cleaning world or, sadly, just goes to work as an employee for some other industry.

The Bottom End pricing does work for some of the larger window cleaning companies. The way these companies use the Bottom End pricing is simple. They already earn great profits from other areas of their service business, so they can afford to work for a ridiculously cheap price or what most window cleaners would consider cheap.

Why almost give the business away? The reason is simple. Large companies may wish to gain control of a new shopping center that's just opening to the public, the low window cleaning prices helps keep competition out. Or, a company recognizes the growing economy in the next town offers their company great potential. Or,

46

a new property manager has begun working for a property management company and you want to get a foothold in the door. The best times for change happens when a property manager is about to leave a company or a new property manager comes on board.

It's tough to raise prices in a falling market. You can only raise prices in a growing local economy.

Ways of increasing profits without raising prices.

Can the windows be cleaned in a quicker, more efficient manner? Sometimes the routes can be made more efficient, or the employees trained to be more efficient with time or given tools that help complete the cleaning in faster time. The Sorbo squeegees with their 36 & 48 inch channels cut down on the time needed to complete many jobs.

If a company has been using ladders to climb up and clean each window, maybe an extension pole or a water-fed pole can be used to speed-up the work while cutting down on labor.

High-rise window cleaning time saving devices are many, but they are also controversial and require a heathly dose of knowledge.

Given the work done and the work still to be completed in the ANSI 839 committee by many competent and dedicated people that help decide what high-rise devices are deemed safe for window cleaners, the high-rise window cleaning innovations will not be discussed at this time. A high level of risk exists in cleaning high-rise where safety is the number one issue.

Window cleaners choosing to set goals to enter the high-rise window cleaning business are strongly recommended to educate themselves in all aspects of high-rise window cleaning.

Another way of increasing profits without increasing prices is to target an area that has the demand for good window cleaning service and the money to pay for it. The poorer the area the less likely a window cleaner will get the price he or she needs to build a professional, high quality business. Sometimes given the circumstances of life, window cleaners may not live in the best residential neighborhoods or towns. Plenty of reputable, experienced window cleaners live in the best neighborhoods and drive the most luxurious cars, but many beginning window cleaners do not have that luxury — yet.

If the community where a window cleaner lives does not support a price level needed to develop a strong company, then window cleaners should take their squeegees, buckets, and poles and test the waters of other communities, valleys, or cities. Staying in one's own community is the easiest and most comfortable decision to make but not always the best in terms of profit and professionalism. Going beyond one's comfort zone to build a window cleaning business where people are willing to pay good money for service may mean the difference between working long days and weeks just to survive or developing a professional company earning what window cleaners deserve: a decent living.

For example: two window cleaners, Tom and Jerry live in the same community: a town of low-income, low-priced affordable housing with high rates of unemployment and government subsidized earnings (welfare).

When Tom moved to this community from another state, he realized immediately that for him to build his business and get the price per hour he felt he needed to survive, he needed to look elsewhere and solicit businesses in other communities, over the mountains in other cities. Tom found an area that was willing to pay the prices he needed not only survive but thrive.

Jerry, on the other hand, felt a little uneasy about traveling over the hills to other cities and decided to stay in his town and try to build a window cleaning business there. Jerry eventually did develop a number of window cleaning accounts, but the pay for his work was much lower than the prices Tom earns for work outside their community.

After a few years of being in business, both window cleaners have developed enough business to earn a living; however, major differences exist between Tom's and Jerry's standard of living. Tom, the one who travels outside the community, drives a new car, takes vacations, and hires people to help him with his work.

Jerry, the one who stays within the community, drives an old car that constantly breaks down, he feels that he can never take a vacation because of his monthly bills, and he has begun to cut corners on his jobs just to get in all his day's work. This is the price one pays for low paying work.

THE
NUTS AND BOLTS
OF BIDDING

"Never assume anything with a customer especially homeowners."

The Wise Window Cleaner

Chapter 4

HOUSE WINDOW CLEANING
—NECESSARY INFORMATION

This chapter takes a look at all the elements that go into house window cleaning bidding: all the factors involved, the types of windows, and the different ways window cleaners approach bidding house windows.

House window cleaning, more than any other window cleaning, has a uniqueness all its own. One of these unique features can best be expressed by a story.

There once was a middle school teacher who taught drama. The teacher had a group of students that wanted to learn but also to enjoy themselves. One day the class practiced on the stage in the cafeteria.

While one group performed, another more mischievous group of students wandered into the kitchen area and explored behind the counters and cooking areas. A custodian finally found the students and brought them back to the class.

The teacher was stunned by where the custodian had found the students. The principal called the teacher about the incident.

When the teacher said, "I just assumed the students would know better than to go into that kitchen area."

The principal leaned forward and said, "Never assume anything especially with middle school students."

I believe the same sage advice goes for the homeowners. Never assume anything with a customer especially homeowners; they can be as interesting as middle school kids.

Homeowners are a different breed of customer from store owners or building property managers. For the most part store owners and building property managers have a tendency to be more reasonable, more businesslike in their dealings — not always but in general. Home owners, especially the owners who hire a window cleaner once every few years, can be slightly to the left of the Twilight Zone.

For instance, a common mistake beginning window cleaners make is to give a homeowner a price for the window cleaning but not to make the services clear enough to the homeowner. When the window cleaner finishes and the homeowner inspects the glass, a window cleaner might hear something about the tracks not cleaned enough, the little spots of paint or hard water stains, or about a scratch on a window. Then the argument begins about whether or not the water stain or calcium deposit removal is considered part of the regular window cleaning.

To the homeowner, yes; he or she wants the stains off the glass. Half the time the stains were the main reason the owner called the window cleaner out in the first place. In this case, the window cleaner didn't tell the owner that hard water removal was not part of the service; he or she just *assumed* the owner would know.

Never assume anything.

Let the homeowner know in writing or at least verbally that water stain removal is an extra charge or that you don't remove water stains or calcium deposits.

Another dispute that can arise is the scratch or scratches on the glass. Windows can be so fogged with dirt that when the wet scrubber moves across the glass the dirt is so thick it feels like wetting sandpaper.

After scrubbing every pane even down into the corners and giving the owner a new view on the world outside, you present the owner with a bill only to find the owner peering at a window with the sun filtering through and noticing a scratch, and here comes the line: "You scratched my windows," or "That scratch wasn't there before." Maybe the owner checks out all the windows and notices more scratches.

Now the homeowner who just the day before couldn't even see out the windows due the build up of dirt is suddenly wanting some type of restitution for a small scratch refracting light. Never assume anything.

Some window cleaners have the homeowner sign a contract that explicitly states that their company is not responsible for scratches found in the glass.

Finally, Rod Woodward, the founder of the American Window Cleaner magazine, told this story: A cardiologist hired Rod to clean the exterior windows on his home in San Francisco. This doctor gave Rod the instructions and then left to go out to lunch with his wife. Rod cleaned the windows, and he finished about the same time the doctor arrived home.

When Rod presented the bill to the doctor, he became upset at the price. Rod had charged $165 for the exterior window cleaning of a mansion. The price did not bother the doctor as much as how short a time it took Rod to clean the windows.

According to the doctor's calculations, the window cleaning price per hour was as much if not more per hour than the doctor made at the time. The doctor could not bring himself to pay more per hour for window cleaning than he himself made as a medical doctor. Since the doctor refused to pay and Rod refused to lower his price, Rod did the only thing he could think of at the time. He went back to every window he cleaned and smeared dirt and mud.

Never assume anything.

Owners want to know the prices up front. In this case, the owner had agreed to the price. The owner's complaint was that the job was completed so quickly that he could not bring himself to pay that much per hour. (Good window cleaners can clean quick, fast, and well.)

When the owner balks at the speed in which the job was completed, some window cleaners try to explain to the customer that the actual window cleaning is just the "tip of the iceberg," the product in a long line of expenses.

For instance, if a window cleaner takes two hours to clean the windows inside and out on a house and charges $100, and if the window cleaner is responsible and takes care of the business side of things, then the window cleaner can explain to the owner that besides cleaning the windows, he or she had to drive to the home site, pay gas, insurance, and depreciation on the vehicle; what happens when the car breaks down? Does the window cleaner factor a percentage for vehicle maintenance? The window cleaner also needed to figure in a portion of other company expenses like liability insurance, advertising, miscellaneous business expenses. After that there's the government taxes: state, local, and federal taxes and social security.

Many window cleaners don't think about taxes until tax time and then the window cleaner's accountant explains that they were supposed to pay estimated quarterly taxes to the government and now they owe thousands of dollars, which the window cleaner, of course, doesn't have in the bank. If the window cleaner has really done the homework, then paying for medical insurance should be a percentage of the hourly rate, too. In today's economy, medical insurance and rising rates are the fastest growning concern for many Americans

After a window cleaner explains the price using those terms, the customer has a better understanding of the business pricing process of window cleaning.

Chapter 5

HOUSE WINDOW CLEANING
— A LOOK AT STRATEGIES FOR
BIDDING HOUSES

Window cleaners are a creative group even when bidding a house. Window cleaners add their own variation and creativity before talking to the homeowner about the price. Some window cleaners offer a discount when window cleaning is requested with other work like gutter cleaning, carpet cleaning, or steam cleaning (three possible add-on businesses that some window cleaning companies like to add). These window cleaners can afford to discount the window cleaning because they make more money on the other services, and, therefore, still earn tremendous profits, maybe even more per window than otherwise expected.

Some window cleaning services like to send out a representative dressed professionally and with great sales ability. These representatives target customers in large homes who are willing to pay $400 and up for window cleaning.

Some companies never go out to the home site to bid the windows. Instead, when the customer calls from the ads placed in the yellow pages, coupon books, and newspapers, they ask the homeowner to count up the number of windows in the house and then they will give him or her an estimate based upon the information, but they make the bid subject to change if the window cleaners get to the house and find the information the homeowner gave to be incorrect.

In many cities with tract houses (the same house built with a few model variations), window cleaners could use this method and, once established and knowledgeable about the housing tracts in the area, the window cleaner can sometimes just ask the owner about the housing tract and the home model and have a good idea of the house layout. For example, the home owner says, "I'm in the Texas tract, the number three floor plan or the largest floor plan." If the window cleaner has done a number of jobs in that tract of homes, then he or she has a good idea of what the job will entail. Sometimes a prospective customer will call up and say, "I got your name from my neighbor; you clean her windows, and I wanted you to bid my windows. I have the same floorplan."

Most window cleaners do travel to the prospective clients home not only to see the home firsthand but to begin to build a relationship with the homeowner. The old saying is true: "You never get a second chance to make a first impression." So good window cleaners put forth a professional image from the moment they meet the homeowner. That professional image would include clean clothes and uniformed shirt (shirt with company logo), the well-groomed and friendly reassuring image. If a window cleaner is trying to earn the most money per hour, then they present themselves in a professional manner.

Homeowners are allowing a stranger into their home. In today's world of craziness, homeowners want to be assured that they're not letting some felon into their home to clean their windows. They want to feel relaxed and secure that the work will be done in a professional manner with the least amount of disruption to the homeowner's lifestyle.

Window cleaners can demonstrate this from the first meeting with the homeowner. A professional window cleaner can put the homeowner at ease and set the tone and attitude of the working relationship with their rapport and knowledge about window cleaning. A customer might ask, "How are you going to get to that window?" as the lady of the house points to a window high on the side of the house or the roof. Or, a homeowner might ask "Can you clean the shower doors, too?" or "Can you remove the water stains?" The answers and tone in which the window cleaner responds help put the homeowner at ease and assure the homeowner that you're worth what you're going to ask for the job.

Security is another big issue with homeowners. As the window cleaner is answering questions, the homeowner is evaluating the window cleaner as to whether or not to allow this person into his or her home. Again, the manner in which the window cleaner presents himself or herself will help dictate whether or not the home owner will decide to accept the bid.

Home window cleaning expenses

Window cleaners that choose house window cleaning have a few more expenses that should be figured into the bid. Remember earlier we talked about window cleaning expenses that customers may not realize when they see the bid.

These expenses or factors incurred by the window cleaner are factors that window cleaners should be aware of so that adjustments can be made in the bidding process. These factors are the bidding time, the cancellation or postponement time, the setup or appointment time, and also a risk factor: ladder and roof work.

Nothing is ever as simple as it seems, and it is true for house window cleaning. House window cleaning should be simple, but in reality it can be more complicated than ever. These four factors are areas few beginning window cleaners consider in the bidding process.

The Bidding Time

Time is money (sorry about the cliche); therefore, time spent soliciting new accounts should be factored into the bid. Salespeople are paid to go out and find new customers. Even window cleaning employees are paid an hourly rate and/or a commission for bringing in new customers. So, does that mean a window cleaner should work for free to get new jobs? Is that factor in the window cleaning bid just a "freebie" to the homeowners? If going out on the job to bid windows is how you solicit new accounts, then factoring in the bidding time should be a percentage of the job. After all, there will be times when no jobs come your way, yet you spent a day or days soliciting new accounts. Each window cleaning bid process can take as little as 15 minutes or longer depending upon the house and homeowner.

Then there is the driving time factor between bidding. When starting out, this bidding process may seem just a part of the job, a necessary evil to get a business started; however, if house window cleaning is going to be a major part of the new business, then running around town bidding windows for no pay may get old quickly. Make sure that a small portion of the bid includes money for time to bid other houses.

Some window cleaners never go out and bid. They bid from their homes at night with the customer on the other end of the telephone line, but this is still a time element.

Cancellations   or   postponements

Nothing, nothing can be more frustrating to the window cleaning business than last minute cancellations or postponements. This is money lost, income not generated, yet the window cleaner still has bills to pay. The bills don't stop coming just because the weather isn't agreeable for window cleaning or the customer decides to take a last minute getaway trip. Another profession that deals with the same problem is dentistry. Dentists have clients cancel at the last minute, too; however, dentists have a built-in cancellation charge if a person cancels too late for the dentist to fill that time slot. Window cleaners seem to just take the loss and move on, yet that is a time slot now where no money will be earned. If the customer is a regular one and pays well, then the postponement may be looked at as just a fact to deal with. If, however, the customer is a constant complainer, lousy payer, and a nightmare job, then consider yourself lucky that they cancelled.

The House Window Cleaning Cycle
House window cleaning in general is cyclical, business goes way up some months of the year and you can't keep up with the work, and a few months later, you can't find enough work to keep you busy.

For example, let's start with the beginning of the year. In general, January, February, and March are traditionally the worst window cleaning months for houses (in the Northern Hemisphere). The homeowner just finished with the holidays, the weather is lousy, and people are busy. Window cleaners scramble to find work, any work. Some window cleaners offer discounts, others incorporate other services into the business that fill the slack in business during the off-season. Still other window cleaners just take the time off as their vacation time.

A young couple in Washington state developed a small but profitable house window cleaning route, but when January, February, and March rolls around, they take off that time to concentrate on their true love: Music. They save enough money working hard during the other nine months of the year to take those cold three months off and practice playing their various musical instruments and listening to good music by the warmth of a wood stove.

Eventually, the weather breaks, the sun shines, people notice their windows and spring cleaning begins. The level of window cleaning business jumps to a respectable one where bills can be paid. The months of April, May, and June begin a renewed sense of business and income.

Then summer hits and people begin the vacation cycle, going out of town for July and August. Or, in September, many customers with children focus more on back to school. The house window cleaning business can fall off slightly to moderately depending upon the customers. Some window cleaners experience no drop-off in business during this time, again, depending upon their customer base. If the clientele or target market is mostly retired senior citizens, then the business drop-off may be none at all.

Before you know it the holidays are back and homeowners panic to get the windows cleaned for the holiday festivities and guests. In October, November, and December, house window cleaning can boom. Everyone wants their windows cleaned immediately. This can cause long days and even longer weeks, but generating the business during the busy months gives the window cleaner the opportunity to save money for the not so good months.

Regular service pricing

Some window cleaners offer customers a deal if the windows can be cleaned on a regular basis even if the weather looks like rain and even if the homeowner isn't home. In Europe, some window cleaners clean the windows on an entire block of houses on a weekly or monthly basis, outside only. Of course the price reflects the service, usually a good discount since the window cleaner doesn't have to go looking for more work or show up at an appointed time or even wait till the sky clears. They just show up rain or shine.

Get paid right away

Even though cleaning house windows can take more planning and more time, the greatest benefit is that the window cleaner is paid immediately. With a check or cash in hand the window cleaner moves on to the next account. This is usually not the case with window cleaning of storefronts or office buildings where the window cleaner must wait sometimes 30, 60, or 90 days for their money.

Set pay schedule

No matter what type of window cleaning you target, set up the paying schedule right from the start. Window cleaning customers can span the entire spectrum of human nature: from behavior that is certifiably crazy to behavior that is professionally polished, from avoiding paying the window cleaning bill to the neurotic who asks you every chance they get if you got paid. Human nature plays out in the grand scheme of dealing with window cleaning customers.

Like a teacher in a classroom that sets the tone and what's expected from the students, the professional window cleaner does much the same thing by setting the tone for the payment schedule. Work should not begin until an agreement is reached as to how the window cleaning will be paid and in which both parties are in agreement as to the service provided. This isn't so much a problem when cleaning house windows. The home owner usually understands that payment is due at the completion of the service.

If you're handing the homeowner a written bid before starting work, include a statement somewhere on the sheet to the effect that payment is due upon completion of the work. Again, setting up how the payment will be made should be agreed upon by both homeowner and window cleaner before starting work. Sometimes homeowners want to pay in advance or just mail a check. Many times homeowners own a business and want the bill sent to their office and have a check sent from accounts receivable. Maybe where the windows are cleaned and where the bill is paid are at two different sites and the window cleaner must drive to another location to get paid. Some window cleaners offer credit card service while others offer barter. Setting up the payment can save a lot of grief and frustation later. How the homeowner wants to pay may not be agreeable to you, and finding out ahead of time can save the window cleaner grief and frustration later.

Minimum Charge

Many window cleaners that clean house windows prefer to offer a minimum charge per house. Some homeowners will call just to have the window cleaner come out and clean a large pane of glass over their sliding door or a window that they can't reach. Or, the home has so few windows that what a window cleaner charges no matter if the bid is by the hour or by the window his or her profit — after driving, unloading equipment, setup and tear-down and drive home— will be in the copper stuff, pennies.

Therefore, to avoid taking a loss in hourly wages, many window cleaners set a minimum charge to go out and clean the few windows or small condominium. This minimum charge is totally up to the individual company and should be based upon a number of factors:

Number one factor: how much does the window cleaner wish to earn per hour? Most window cleaners set a goal to earn a certain wage per hour. This hourly rate depends on the area, the competition, and the mindset of the window cleaner. All three factors play a role in the decision about a minimum charge; however, the decision still comes down to how much do you want to make an hour every day you walk out the door?

To go out to a house site, even a small house or condominium, most window cleaners will blockout at least an hour's worth of time even for a small job that could take them as little as 15 minutes to clean, but by the time they arrive, setup, clean and tear down, at least an hour will be consumed. That's an hour's wage lost cleaning two windows or just a few windows (This does not include windows with a high degree of difficulty: high "roof walking" windows or those windows above the two-story levels.) So, how much are you worth an hour?

As of this writing, most window cleaners earn at least $50 per hour or more. If you say you're worth at least $50 per hour then the minimum charge for a house call would be at least $50, and you would let the homeowner know upfront the minimum charge for service.

One window cleaner used his minimum charge as a way of advertising in the local paper. Since many houses in his city were small suburban homes, he placed an ad as follows:

> Window Cleaning
> Most homes $50.

The $50 price was the minimum price he used to go out on the job. This particular window cleaner bid house windows by the window pane, so, he counted up the windows and if the total amount surpassed the minimum charge, then he explained why he needed to charge a higher price. Most reasonable homeowners accepted the reality of the price for the service, but the window cleaning ad's low price motivated the homeowner to call in the first place.

Now if the driving time is even farther then usual, and you still want to do the job — many window cleaners would decline the job unless it's really important — then they figure in the driving time to and from the job even for a minimum job.

69

"Every customer has their price."

The Wise Window Cleaner

Chapter 6

INSPECTING THE HOME

There are many factors that window cleaners will take into consideration while inspecting the window cleaning needs of a home. Some factors will not apply and others will, but knowing all the variables that can happen when bidding houses will hopefully save you some potential grief later.

Driving time
How far are you willing to travel for work? When bidding house windows, customers will call in from many different areas, and good window cleaning companies know their distance limitations or what to charge for house window cleaning outside these limitations—
for house bidding, know your limits.

If a homeowner calls, saying that you were recommended highly and wants you to bid her condominium windows, but she lives in the next town 25 miles away, what would you say?

One window cleaner received a call from a person leaving the country and wanted their house windows cleaned for a tenant that would be arriving shortly. One problem — the house was over an hour's drive from the window cleaner's home. The window cleaner explained that he would have to charge the homeowner for driving time since it was so far. The homeowner said that was not a problem. The window cleaner got the job and money for the driving time as well. In some cases the homeowner will not pay for driving time. Are you willing to go past your driving limit to clean a house, and if so, do you know what you would charge?

The layout of the home

Such a variety of floor plans of homes exists. Floor plans can make a difference in the pricing of the window cleaning. Take House A and House B as examples.

In House A rooms are wall-to-wall windows (5-15 windows per room) easy to get to and a lot of window cleaning can be accomplished in a short amount of time in that room.

House B has only one window per room and you have to lug your bucket, find a place to set it down, wring out the scrubber, wash the window, then put everything back into the bucket and move on to the next room.

In House A the number of windows you can clean in an hour would be double compared to House B. House A's windows are grouped together, three, four, or more windows in same room while in House B's windows, you have one window per room which means more time.

Another factor is the reachability of the inside windows. Even though windows are on the first floor of the house, windows can still be way out of reach. With all the cathedral ceilings in new houses today, window cleaners need a ladder for many inside windows. Ladder work inside the home takes the most time since extra care must be taken not to scratch the paint or wallpaper or drip dirty water on the wall.

The type and size of the windows

Many standard window sizes exist; The term "standard"— used loosely here for windows seen most often in the window cleaner's town or city — offers window cleaners a chance to categorize and simplify the bidding process. Look at the windows in any town and eventually you begin to pick out certain types of windows used most often. Windows can be super large (4'x8' and larger), super small (little diamond-shaped glass that's beveled and only 2 inches in width), and everything else in between.

To attempt to standardize a pricing structure for all the sizes and shape, would only complicate the bidding process; however, windows can be categorized into groups depending upon what works for the window cleaner.

Some window cleaners will judge the job by the length of time necessary to clean the specific types of windows. That will vary depending upon the window cleaner. Each works at a different speed. As you clean the various windows, you can begin to gauge a per window time.

Are the screens new or old?

Old screens can feel fused with the window frame and no amount of tapping and prodding can release the screen. Dirt, rain and sun all play a part in sticking the screens to the window frames making screen removal difficult. If the house is old, check the screens and see how hard it will be to remove them. Some screen hardware is so old that it falls apart when you attempt screen removal. Will you have to come back and fix screen hardware or will you just write a note on the bid about not responsible for screen hardware and explain it to the owner before you start?

Are the screens fastened to the window frame by other means?

Sometimes the screen doesn't fit the window properly and the homeowner attaches the screen with screws which means every window screen would need to be unscrewed and reattached. This process is time intensive.

Are the screens security screens?

A delicate and risky-to-clean screen, these screens set-off an alarm when cut. Interwoven within the screen material is a thread spaced a few inches apart throughout the screen.

The screens are plugged in at the base and all of them are connected. The major problem isn't the removal; the security screens are easy enough to remove. It's the plugging and unplugging that causes some screens to stop working and then the homeowner wants you to fix the problem.

Security screens can be brushed gently but not washed. Extra time and care are needed.

Are the screens removed from inside the house or from outside the house?

Why is screen removal time important? Screens that can be removed from outside the house take less time to remove and put back, while screens that must be removed from the inside can be a labor-intensive job taking twice as much time to remove and put back.

The screen that can be removed from the outside can be "popped out" and the window cleaner can just move along the wall to the next screen and around the house until all the screens are removed. Or, the window cleaner may prefer to "pop" the screen, brush it, clean the window, and replace the screen. (Some homeowners just want the screens brushed.)

Screens removed from the inside take time

Screens that must be removed from inside the house, require extra time and effort. Here is where many window cleaners get into trouble: they try to remove a screen from the outside that should be removed from the inside, and what happens is they force the screen out bending the screen causing major damage.

Screens that must be removed from the inside require the laborious process of going through the house, through each room and opening the windows and attemping to pop the screen out to the inside and then dropping it on the outside for cleaning. The alternative is to go tramping through the house with dusty, dirty screens and then depositing them outside.

The worst case scenario is that the screen can't be removed unless the window is popped out also. This might happen more often than you can imagine. You have to slide the window to find the point where the window pops out, lift the all-too-often heavy window out of the tracks, set the window down, then pop the screen out, and then either find a place to put the window or place the window back in the tracks. This process takes time to accomplish and can take as much as three times longer than removing a window from the outside.

How can you tell if a screen can be removed from the outside or should be removed from the inside?

Here's a tip to see if a screen can be taken off from the outside or inside. Stand outside in front of a window with a screen. Now, look at the four borders of the screen. If you can see the two sides of the screen completely or top and bottom edges clearly with little of the window framing blocking them, then the screen should be able to be removed from the outside.

When the two exposed metal moldings are the sides of the screen, then you push up on the top of the screen or pry the bottom of the screen with a flat piece of metal (screwdriver or even a household butter knife) to pop the screen out of its track.

When the two exposed metal moldings are the top and bottom of the screen, then you push on one of the sides away from the other side or pry one side with a flat piece of metal.

If you can't see any of the sides clearly and the window frame is obstructing all four sides of the screen even partially, then the screen must be removed from the inside.

How much dirt buildup on the outside?

Are the sills caked with dirt and dust? Are the windows so dirty that no amount of water will clean the window the first time? Chances are that the window will need to be washed more than once and the bucket of water will be so black after a few windows that it will need to be changed every few windows.

Do the windows have any paint spots or overspray?

A few windows with some paint would not be unusual for a house, and you can talk with the homeowner about whether removing the paint spots is important.

When a majority of windows are covered with lots of paint overspray or paint drips, then the window cleaning begins to fall into another type of window cleaning: Post Construction Cleanups which is another type of bidding process. Post Construction Cleanups can be a major headache if you do not know what you are doing. Time consuming tasks and the risk of damaging glass are two major reasons to look seriously at whether you want to clean one of these jobs if you are new to the business.

Do the windows have hard water spots?

The hard water stains may be a big reason the owner called you out in the first place.

Rub a wet finger over a small area of the window you suspect contains hard water spotting. The spots will not come off with just water. They may feel raised up or bumpy. The hard water spotting is caused by ground water hitting the window over time. Lawn sprinklers are the major cause of water hitting the windows and leaving hard water spots. Are you ready and willing to clean them or are you going to say that you do not clean hard water stains from the windows? Talk to the homeowner about the stains.

If you are not prepared to clean the spots, let the homeowner know. Some window cleaners never want to add water stain removal as part of the window cleaning. Others know that water stain removal can triple the price of cleaning that window. If you decide to learn water stain removal, study the cleaning solutions that work. Do not go into the cleaning of water stains without some knowledge of the process.

Is there a smoke or heavy dirt buildup on the inside glass?

The windows in the home of a heavy smoker can be particularly challenging. Smoke— any kind of smoke— clings to glass panes. Smoke buildup does not take long to form. Even one cigarette can leave noticeable deposits on the window. Smoke on windows slows the window cleaning. More water and cleaning solution are needed and "fanning" or the "S-method" of squeegeeing the glass leaves residue. Just pulling the squeegee straight across the glass prevents residue marks. Cleaning smoky windows takes more time, maybe even twice as long to clean each window.

How much dust and dirt buildup on the inside?

When the windows haven't been cleaned in a while and dirt and dust have built up, the windows appear to have a film on them; when you rub your hand on the glass, it feels like fine sandpaper. When you wet a window heavy with dirt and dust, it makes a sound like sandpaper on wood. These windows take more time.

Are the windows tinted?

In sunny regions, homeowners cover the inside window with a type of clear laminate tint to help block out sun rays. Some tints are easy to work with not slowing the window cleaning and not scratching easily and no accommodations need to be made for the tint.

With other tints, cheap tints that scratch easily, extra care must be taken to make sure not to scratch the tint. Some tints will scratch with even the softest window scrubber. Some window cleaners use a baby's cotton diaper on these tinted windows. Other cheap tints actually bind up the squeegee as it moves across the glass. These cheap tints need extra care when cleaning. First explain to the homeowner that fine scratch lines may appear in the tint even if the softest scrubbing material is used. Then check the windows with the sunlight streaming through the window to make sure the cleaning process is not causing any major scratch lines.

Will you have to scrape paint from windows or debris from the glass?

The removal of fine paint overspray or any

paint drops, stucco, decals, or tape will occasionally need to be removed from windows. Sometimes the scraping needed is minor sometimes major. How much scraping — if any — would be required? Window cleaners concentrating on post construction cleanups will earn five times or more per window because scraping takes time and carries a higher degree of risk than just straight window cleaning. Every window with material to be scraped will take time.

What is the layout of the ground around the home?

The terrain around the perimeter of the house can add more time and even risk to the window cleaning. In general most homes sit on level ground; however, with that level ground can be problems.

What obstacles lay in the way of the window cleaning?

Here are just a few obstacles:

• A patio roof that creates a problem for reaching second story windows or is too unstable to support any weight from the window cleaner.

• Trees or bushes that obstruct or lie in the path needed to get to the window.

• Fences that must be walked around or climbed over with a ladder and other equipment.

• Other buildings or structures obstructing windows to be cleaned.

Does the ground slope away from the house?

When the ground around the house is unlevel or sloped, then another set of time wasters comes into play. When the ground slopes away from the house creating a nightmare for window cleaners using a ladder, then extra time is needed to secure the footings for the ladder. One tip suggested years ago in the American Window Cleaner Magazine recommends digging two holes in the ground, one for each ladder leg to support the ladder. Again, this adds time to the job. Sometimes digging holes isn't possible, so an extra person would be needed to hold the ladder, making sure it doesn't slip while from the window cleaner is washing the window.

Another possibility is to purchase ladder levelers. These handy devices attach to the base of each ladder leg and each one adjusts or extends to compensate for the unlevel ground. These ladder levelers are a welcome edition to any window cleaner's tools; however, even ladder levelers take time to adjust so that the ladder leans at a proper angle against the wall.

If the ground is such that the ladder still will be unsteady then, again, another person will be needed for the job and that's more time.

Check the Occupational Safety and Health Administration, OSHA, for guidelines to using ladders on the job or any safety issues. Some states insist that another person be at the bottom of the ladder to help stabilize it.

How many times will a ladder have to be moved?

Some window cleaners count the number of times they will have to move the ladder, and they add time to those windows. Moving, climbing, and cleaning the window using a ladder can double or triple the time necessary to clean the window. Also, there is a certain inherent risk in ladder work. Some windows are extra wide and a ladder must be moved twice for each window. Or, a "ladder stand-off" can be purchased that holds a ladder centered over a window so a window can be cleaned from the front instead of the sides of the window.

How much time will be needed in moving equipment or getting to a window?

Some houses appear set up with more obstacles than the Normandy Landing during World War II. Everywhere the homeowner has fences, dog runs, storage bins, more gates and fences. Maybe a swimming pool or pond is right where you need to place a ladder. What obstacles will slow down the window cleaning?

Will extra care be needed inside the home?

You walk into some homes and right away you know it's not an ordinary house: antiques up against the windows, shoes must be removed upon entering the house, a carpet that's whiter than snow, stuff piled high in rooms, any of these obstacles and more can signal that the house will take extra time.

Probably the most time consuming item, though, will be the window coverings. Here a wide array of products decorate the window for the homeowner and obstruct the glass.

Sometimes the window coverings are easy: miniblinds that you just pull up out of the way or drapes that pull open. Other times the window coverings are elaborate and ornate coverings that become the window cleaners worst nightmare. Wood shutters can take an inordinate amount of time to open out of the way and close. Little obstructions to the shutters can make the window cleaning difficult. Sheer window coverings, lacy, fine and easily stained, must be dealt with in a manner so they're not damaged. Sometimes this means that they must be removed, otherwise the dirt from the window water will stain an expensive item.

Usually, though, it's a combination of window coverings. Not only does the homeowner have the fine lacy coverings, but also miniblinds or some other covering so the window cleaner is pulling off layers of material just to get to a window. Multiply this times every window in the house and this all adds time to the job.

What type of homeowner personality are you dealing with?

While the homeowner questions and evaluates you before contracting the window cleaning, a window cleaner should be evaluating the homeowner before accepting the job. The personality of homeowners can range over the entire spectrum of human personality. Just when you thought you've seen it all, another homeowner surprises you.

Most homeowners, about 80 percent, actually are kind, level-headed people that follow the Golden Rule (Treat others the way you would want to be treated.) The other twenty percent live on the fringes of personality and those are the customers to watch. Not that a window cleaner can put a price on the personality of the homeowner, but observing the homeowner or listening to what the homeowner says and how they say it, may tip you off to unrealistic expectations about how they want you to clean the windows or to the extraordinary amount of extras they want done for the same price.

Some homeowners are overly demanding. For example, they want the window tracks vacuumed out or excessively cleaned. Or, the homeowner wants towels laid down on the window sills on all the windows just before any window cleaning. This type of service is not the norm, but can be provided by the window cleaner, but hopefully, he or she charges more for the service.

The worst type, though, is the homeowner that follows the window cleaner, watching every step, every window and inspects the window when it's done. These people are usually the same homeowners that get their windows cleaned every 10 years, so the windows are filthy. Then about every few windows they'll say, "You missed a spot." Or the homeowner is so cheap that the price negotiated is far lower than the window cleaner realized.

To be honest, putting a price on homeowners' personalities has no professional basis. It's just something that the window cleaner may use if so desired. For instance, if the window cleaner realizes in talking to the homeowner that the homeowner will make the job a nightmare or be overly demanding in what service they want for the money, then the window cleaner has two choices: either turn down the job or boost the bid price.

Occasionally, walking away from the job is best. One window cleaner bid a house and after giving the price to the homeowner, the homeowner began to pull the bid apart criticizing the price and arguing that there were not that many windows and that the job wasn't that hard and then, almost in the same breath, asked for other things to be done for the same price. A warning signal went off in the window cleaner's head that this customer would be terrible to deal with, so the window cleaner politely said he would not be able to do the job and recommended a few competitors in the area. The man began to insist that the window cleaner stay and negotiate a price. The window cleaner politely said he had to leave and wished the homeowner luck.

Most homeowners are nice, relaxed, and trusting people. The window cleaner can go about the business of washing windows with little supervision or inspection; a certain amount of trust is given and the professional window cleaner keeps that trust.

What adjustments to the cleaning need to be made?
Once the window cleaner has inspected the house, what services does the homeowner request?

Does the homeowner want all the windows cleaned?

Just the outside?

Just the second floor?

Scrape off paint or stickers?

Remove hard water stains or screen burn?

Clean the mirrors?

What about screen cleaning? Will the screens be brushed or washed?

The tracks cleaned out?

Looking at just the potential questions to be answered can intimidate the beginning window cleaner.

The variables are many and carry with them a high learning curve but eventually the process becomes organized and easier to manage.

The Price of Underbidding a Job

Underbidding a job carries with it terrible effects. Once you start checking your time on the job and realize the job is going much slower than you thought it would take, you may take a few different stances. One way is to just tell yourself you learned a lesson and you won't underbid a job like than one again and continue to clean in the highest professional manner possible.

William J. O'Neal, founder and publisher of *Investment Business Daily*, says it another way: When you don't get the expected results, you chalk it up as an educational expense. You pay to go to school. Just view the income lost as an educational expense and that you have learned the lesson, and you won't have to pay for it again — hopefully.

If you are not one of those window cleaners that will chalk this money-losing job up to
getting an education, then a few options exist:

You decide the job is way more than you
thought it would be andyou back out of the job
— not professional but a choice.

You begin to take shortcuts to decrease
your time and increase your profits; you find
ways to maybe not clean a window because it
looks clean. That screen that didn't come off
easily you just leave. No one can tell that the
window hasn't been cleaned, so just forget it.
If the homeowner really says something about
it, then you'll go back and clean it.

There are all sorts of little, unprofes-
sional tricks you can use. Hopefully, you don't
lower your professionalism to that level.

As you can see, many variables can add to
the cost and time of house window cleaning —
more so than any other type of window cleaning. Each owner creates a home unique to his
or her personality and in doing so also creates
unique set of challenges to cleaning the windows
in that home. The better you understand these
possible challenges, the better you will be at pre-
senting a competitive but profitable bid to the
owner.

Chapter 7

BIDDING HOUSE WINDOWS

In this chapter we will cover the bidding strategies used by most window cleaners, the six methods possible for house window cleaning. Review all of them before making your choice. Each has its own merits and place in the bidding process depending on your region, your needs, and your customer's needs. These methods are not the absolute final word about bidding but a starting place. As you gain experience, you will adjust your bid pricing.

The house window cleaning methods to be covered are the following:

bidding by the hour
by the day

by the house
by the entire window
by the window pane
or a combination of the above.

Bidding by the hour

Bidding by the hour means calculating the time you spend on a particular job and then multiplying that time by the per hour dollar rate you wish to earn. Calculating the amount of time you spend for a job can including any or all of the following activities:

driving out to the house
speaking with the homeowner

OUTSIDE THE HOUSE
walking the perimeter of the house
counting the number of windows that
can be cleaned without a ladder
counting the number of windows that
need to be cleaned with a ladder
(walking the roof counts as ladder
work -- higher risk pays more)
checking the type of windows
checking for hard water stains
checking for damaged glass
checking the type of screens
checking the slope of the land
checking for obstacles

INSIDE THE HOUSE
counting windows that need a ladder
checking for obstacles blocking windows
checking the window coverings and sills
for excessive amounts of objects that
need to be moved.
Extras the owner needs completed (closet
and bathroom mirrors, hard water stain
removal)

Bidding house window cleaning by the hour takes experience. However, in the long run, all of these ways of bidding — by the hour by the house, by the window, by the pane, ultimately come down to how much do you want to earn an hour, or day? And, how much are homeowners willing to pay for services?

Many window cleaners with a few hundred houses under their belt, understand explicitly how long a job is going to take. After all, learning what works and doesn't work takes time.

The best reason for bidding by the hour is that a window cleaner can walk around the house and plan out how to wash the windows by looking at all the different variables that are mentioned in the previous chapter. Once done the experienced window cleaner will have a pretty good idea how long the job will take.

The positive side To bidding by the hour.

On the positive side, going out to bid the home gives the homeowner the opportunity to meet the window cleaner. This time spent with the homeowner gives the window cleaner a chance to be a salesperson, explaining to the homeowner the window cleaning service that he or she would provide and why the homeowner should use their service.

A few large window cleaning companies on the East Coast send out sales representatives to the large mansions. These cleancut, uniformed individuals actually sell the service as much as bid the service.

Another positive is that the window cleaner views first hand what the job will entail. Most houses have similar window cleaning needs, but a few will have some peculiarity: bars on the windows, really high or really difficult-to-get-to windows, or more. By going to the job, the window cleaner can gauge firsthand what the job will take.

In a few cases, window cleaners just tell the homeowner what their hourly rate will be and however long the job takes, well, that's what the the price would be.

They can "guesstimate" what it will take, but they get to work at their pace without fear of going below the hourly rate they wish to earn.

Drawbacks to bidding hourly

One of the potential drawbacks of bidding hourly is that the window cleaner must go out to look at the job. This costs time and money. In the small house market this does not always make sense. When a homeowner calls for a bid, the window cleaner must go out and bid the house in person. Yes, you can attempt to sell the homeowner on the cleaning, but in some cases another window cleaner will win the job and you're out the time and energy spent chasing that one.

In some towns, this process would not be a big deal; in other towns, though, with miles and miles between point A and point B, this would eat away at the time during the day plus add miles to the car expenses.

If the house jobs in that area are small, under $100, then bidding by the hour may not make sense because the amount of time taken to bid costs too much time and money.

The key to good hourly bidding is planning. If you're a beginning window cleaner, then you'll go bid at any time, but if you already have an established route, then planning is important so as not to waste any time.

Set aside times of the day, like late afternoons or early evenings, to do your bidding. Maybe you prefer bidding during the hottest times of the day when you can't work anyway or whenever rain washes out your scheduled houses for that day. You can still bid the jobs. Or, choose a day to go bid when your driving distance to the bid will be the closest. Tell the potential customer that you'll be in the area on Tuesday and ask if it is all right to stop in then.

Another potential problem with hourly bidding is that the bidding becomes subjective. The window cleaner is guessing how long the job will take given the variables (number of windows, layout of the ground and house, etc.).

Some window cleaners are overly optimistic by nature. They'll look at a job and feel confident that they'll be able to complete the job in four hours when the actual time will be five hours. On almost every job they do, they underestimate the time it will take to clean the windows. If you are one of these people, optimistic about everything, then either learn to add time to your estimated cleaning time or use one of the other methods for bidding.

The final potential problem with hourly bidding is that it can leave the window cleaner vulnerable to customer questioning. Sometimes the customer will question the bid and how long the job will take in an effort to lower the price.

Or, they will mention another window cleaner's bid because it's lower, and they want you to do the job for the other guy's price. When the window cleaner has figured by the hour, then all he or she has is the "gut feeling" of how long the job will take to clean. Working with a customer that wants a lower price or a better understanding as to why the price is what they consider high, can be difficult. It can be done though.

Bidding by the hour, judging how long the job will take, now comes under attack and the only evidence you have is your good judgment, but most window cleaners won't value their judgment; they value the homeowners judgment and start a process of discounting the bid. After all, the goal is to get the job. Right? The answer is "maybe." Too many other factors exist .

Murphy's Law

Murphy's Law: Whatever can go wrong will go wrong, or whatever is planned will take longer and cost more than expected. Something to think about when bidding the job by the hour.

Bidding by the day

Used by larger companies with employees this method allows a window cleaner the opportunity to generate a daily income even though the job is not a whole day.

If a house is going to take 3/4 of a day to clean the windows, should you or would you charge for the full day since you're not going to get another house in before the sun sets?

Some window cleaning companies in Japan bid the job by the day since by the time the workers arrived to the job, did the job and left, not enough time existed to send the workers out again on another job. The owner still must pay a per diem wage for the window cleaner, so to avoid losing that money, the owner of the window cleaning company charges the customer for a day's worth of window cleaning, and since the owner sets a goal to make that certain amount per day, he or she just charges the customer the daily rate. This method is used with bidding commercial office buildings but can be used for bidding mansions or large difficult houses.

Bidding by the house

In some locations around the country, the houses are built all the same with just a few variations in the floor plan.

Condominiums can fit this description, too. A complex of condos all identical with a few variations of the window placements and floor plans or sizes: studios, one-bedrooms, two-bedrooms, and three-bedroom floor plans.

When you clean enough houses with the same floor plan, then similar prices begin to appear on the bids. You know how long the job will take given nothing unusual was added to the house or obstructing the windows, and an initial bid can be given right over the phone.

With condomiums you can post signs around the complex stating how much for each floor plan. This is a general rule of thumb and not hard and fast. Some variations do exist.

Bidding by the entire window

Certain areas of the country have homes

with similar types of windows whether they are double-hung or two-pane sliders. The sizes will vary within the house from 4-feet by 8-foot sliding doors to small bathroom windows.

When bidding by the entire window, the price is the same for all the windows. This simplifies the bidding process for the window cleaner and homeowner.

The most common question that arises from the homeowner is why should they pay the same price for the large sliding doors and the small bathroom windows? The answer is that the bid per window is an average price taking into account all the windows and sizes.

So, while the sliding door is larger, the bathroom window is smaller and makes up for the extra time needed to clean the sliding doors. Some homeowners might say they do not want the small bathroom window cleaned. In that case you need to explain the per window pricing that includes the bathroom window or charge more for the larger windows.

Usually, two prices exist, one for first floor windows and another for second. The first floor has no ladder work usually and therefore should take less time to clean. Second story windows usually involve ladder work or removing windows or roof walking. This time, effort and risk should be compensated in a way that allows you to earn the maximum hourly amount. Business is about making money. Prices vary but doubling the single story window price for second story windows and first floor windows that need ladder work is not uncommon.

Advantages to bidding by the window

In certain regions of the country and city suburbs, bidding by the window is a simplified approach to window cleaning; so much so that a window cleaner can actually discuss the price to clean the windows over the phone. The window cleaner can choose to go out and look at the windows, but this simple approach allows window cleaners and homeowners to get a rough estimate before any window cleaning begins. The window cleaner asks the homeowner how many windows he or she has in the home. The homeowner might know already, count from memory around the house or just tell the window cleaner that they will call back. The window cleaner doesn't have to waste time and money going out to the home and earns the business right over the phone. It's important, though, that the window cleaner state clearly that the bid is a tentative bid based upon the information given.

SAMPLE PRICES

The following price guide is to give window cleaners a starting point for bidding house windows. With experience, a window cleaner will adjust the pricing structure to fit his or her needs.

First floor windows (cleaned without a ladder)

Sliding 3-foot by 4-foot windows $8-$12	per window set
French windows	.50 per pane
Louvered (jalousie) windows	$1-$2 per pane
Storm windows	$15 - $25 per set

Second floor windows (and first floor ladder work)

Sliding 3-foot by 4-foot windows $10-$15	per window set
French windows	.90 per pane
Louvered (jalousie) windows	$1-$2 per pane
Storm windows	$20-$30 per set

Disadvantages to bidding by the window

So many styles of windows exist today that it's hard to lump all windows into just a few categories. It would be simple if all windows came in a few standard sizes for all houses, but the reality is that our country promotes individualism, creativity, and ingenuity; therefore, not all windows are created equally; in fact anything but common sizes and shapes appears to be the norm.

This method doesn't work well for small cut-ups or French windows or windows with more than two "lites" or panes per window.

Bidding by the window pane

Many window cleaners choose to bid by the window pane because of the wide variety of windows that exist today. There are two approaches to this type of bidding.

The first approach simplifies the bidding by making one price for each window if the largest window in the house is the sliding glass door. Even though the sliding doors are four by six foot panes, the bathroom window is much smaller and makes up for the sliding doors. So the window cleaner or the owner counts all the windows and from that a rough estimate can be obtained.

First floor windows are one price and second floor windows plus hard-to-reach first story windows another price.

You create your own pricing structure per window. The example gives you a look at how this bidding method works. These prices are general prices that may work in your area or may be low or high for your area.

Some window cleaners want to know the square footage of the house, giving the window cleaner an estimate of the amount of walking between windows.

SAMPLE HOUSE

A house contains 15 sliding windows, two panes each including a sliding glass door and two french doors with 10 panes each on the first floor. On the second floor, there are 10 sliding windows with two-panes each and two more windows with three panes each.

The bid for the window cleaning would be as follows:

First floor

Sliding windows
30 panes at $2.50 per pane = $75.00
French windows
20 panes at .50 per pane   = $10.
First floor total $85.00

Second Floor
Sliding windows
22 panes at $5.00 per pane = $110.00

Total for both floors   = $195.00

Advantages to bidding by the pane

Bidding by the window pane has many advantages. One major advantage is that it allows the window cleaner to give a rough estimate over the phone asking the homeowner the number of windows and any other information you need.

Another advantage is that when bidding by the window pane, the bidding is more specific. The homeowner may not like the price and question the price, but all the window cleaner needs to emphasize is that the owner has "X" number of window panes and the price charged per pane is "X" dollars. Bidding by the pane makes standing by the quote much easier.

Finally, bidding by the window pane gives the window cleaner the flexibility to adjust the prices to reflect the size of the pane. With all the custom windows in homes today, window cleaners can create certain price structures to reflect these different windows.

Disadvantages to bidding by the pane

Some homeowners may feel confused by the pricing structure: counting window panes, wondering how large a French window would be or how small is a regular window.

Another disadvantage is that bidding over the phone is hard to sell to the owners of large homes or mansions. These owners do not have time to go around their 5,000 square-foot house counting windows. To them it's your job. You may lose a good potential customer by asking them to count the windows in their mansion.

A combination of the bidding choices

Though many window cleaners choose one particular method of bidding, some choose a combination of methods. For instance, one possible combination might be bidding by the window pane, but you have a set price for bay windows. Or you have a set price for sets of storm windows and a window pane price for all other windows.

Comparing or Cross-referencing Bidding Choices

A good idea is to compare two different ways of bidding. A common method is to calculate a price on a per window basis, and then walk the job again considering the job on an hourly basis. How do the bids compare? If there are five or more windows in each room, the job will go much faster per window than if there are three or less windows per room and more walking is needed. You might be able to give a more competitive price with the hourly rate especially on a larger home.

An exercise for new window cleaners

If you are thinking of getting into the business or just starting to get into the trade, then try this exercise. Wherever you are living now clean your windows.

Before you begin, write down the time you make the decision to clean the windows. Then go get the equipment out of the garage or closet and set up for cleaning the windows. Remove the screens as you clean or all at one time — that's your choice, but don't clean the screens during this window cleaning. Concentrate on just cleaning glass. Clean all the windows at a pace that allows you to do the best job on cleaning, and when you finish and all the screens are back on the windows and the bucket and squeegee are back where they were stored, then and only then write down the time it took to clean the windows.

> How long did cleaning your own windows take you?
> How many windows did you clean per hour?
> How much did you want to earn per hour?

The first time you clean any window cleaning job will be the longest time and effort you will spend on that job. When you clean the windows a second time, figure on cutting the time it takes by about 25%, sometimes more. So don't be too hard on yourself if you feel you spent too much time.

Advice from Three Pros in the Business

Norm Popp, Santa Barbara Window Cleaning

In our area, we have many custom-built homes, none of which follows a standard size or shape.

First, I have an average per pane window price that I charge. The per pane price is comprised of labor and overhead plus profit, based on the average number of windows that can be cleaned in an hour. We try to keep the system fairly simple. Prices vary for the first floor and second floor windows. Also, the price varies whether the window is a French or regular window, etc.

Second, I walk the job and estimate how long I would take based on my experience. I take into consideration access to the windows, tricky ladder work, excessive dirt, water spots, plastic tint, screen removal, and other factors. Then, I estimate a ballpark seat-of-the-pants number of hours (again using my labor and overhead plus profit number).

I compare the number of hours with the basic price. If it appears there are no complicating factors, I stick with the basic price (or slightly discounted if the job is really easy). If the job looks difficult, I will estimate the price based more on my experience and raise the basic price to cover the additional expenses of a difficult job. If a customer states they want regular service, I will discount the price, but not until we schedule and clean the second time. Too many customers claim they want regular services, then never have you back.

Steven Miller, Great Lakes Window Cleaning

The house windows in our area are similar. Basically, there are four types of windows built into these houses. Occasionally, a potential customer calls with a custom home, but that's not the norm.

We bid mostly by phone. Driving to homes

to bid is too time consuming. We find utilizing the phone the most efficient means of bidding houses. When a potential customer calls, we ask them the area in which they live. This gives us an idea of the driving time. There is only so much travel time we allow. Most of our work is within a half-hour's drive of the office.

Since there are only four types of windows, we ask them to describe their window style. We help them describe their windows, asking questions ranging from how the window looks to how many panes in each window to how the window opens. Next, we ask them to count the number of windows in their home, first and second floor.

Once we have the home's location, the number of windows, and the type of windows then, we quote the owner a price. We never tell our customer the per window price.

We do not separate first floor from second floor windows; the price is the same for both.

Jon Capon, Capon Building Services
(Now president of Valcourt Building Services)

Our area is full of large custom and colonial homes. We have very few "row" homes and condominiums. We go to the door to bid the jobs.

We could give a bid over the phone when the homeowners look for quotes, but then we don't want to lose the job to a competitor.

Our representatives go face-to-face with the potential customers. That way the customer gets to see us and our company. The image we really want to project is one of trust. Sure, customers want competitive prices. But, more than that they want window cleaners in their homes they can trust and be professional. Our brochure helps us project an air of professionalism.

By going directly to the customer's door, we sell 9 out of 10 jobs.

When bidding the windows, we use a per pane price. Starting with a base price for ground floor work, we raise the per pane price for each floor. We don't deviate from these per pane bids. We figure some jobs will take a little more time than others, but it will all balance out. Sometimes the job is unusual like a customer needs two fourth floor windows cleaned and we need a 40-foot ladder. That's different, then we adjust the price accordingly.

Chapter 8

STOREFRONT WINDOW CLEANING

Storefront window cleaning covers a wide range of buildings. Virtually, any nonresidential building, usually one story, can be classified as a storefront. They would include all retail stores, banks, gas stations, automotive repair or dealers, restaurants and even the small manufacturing businesses located in business parks.

Many storefronts are located in shopping centers and malls, but a large portion of these accounts can be found in other areas often overlooked by window cleaners. Some storefronts are actually converted homes where the zoning laws changed from residential to commercial. Other storefronts are found at the airport or golf course.

Sun, wind, rain or snow, the storefront window cleaner is in business. You may wonder how storefront window cleaners can work in the rain, but most storefronts have overhangs that protect the windows from the rain.

Storeowners usually want clean windows so the product they sell will be the most presentable to customers and potential customers. Clean windows in a store also presents an image of cleanliness in the establishment. It sets the tone for customers walking into the store.

Storefronts, however, are popular. One reason is that you can show up on your schedule instead of setting up an appointment for window cleaning as you do with houses and office buildings. Scheduling appointments for, window cleaning like those for houses, takes time. Storefronts offer tremendous flexibility if established right.

The storefront window cleaning bidding, in many ways, is different from all other types of window cleaning bidding. In some ways it resembles the board game Monopoly, especially in a new shopping center. Window cleaners converge on the new stores trying to be the first to sell the new owner a service. The players are all the window cleaners bidding windows in that shopping center. The object of the game is the same as Monopoly: How many storefronts (properties) can you acquire? Who will be the first to sell the owner on a window cleaning service? One competitor solicits new work with a "If I get the job, great, if not, that's okay" attitude while another competitor may solicit as if his life depended upon getting the job. You are apt to be more successful in the storefront business if you go after each account as though the game depended upon it. Sometimes allowing a competitor to get even one job in the same center means trouble. The window cleaner with the most storefronts usually earns the most income and highes per hour rate. Afterall, they can spend more time in one center and less time driving.

Storefront window cleaning in the most competitive cities shows the free enterprise system at its best. With so many window cleaners knocking on doors one's price floats to the level to match the competition. So when bidding storefronts, you should have a feel already for what the storefront market in your area will bear.

By asking storeowners what they pay, you can get a feel for the going rate in that area. One town might be extremely low-paying while the town just over the hill pays very well. It just depends on the market.

No one can be efficient in the storefront business with just one store in each shopping center (unless that storefront earns at least an hour's wage); it's an economic disaster waiting to happen. A window cleaner needs at least three jobs or more in one shopping center to make cleaning storefronts in the center workable.

Are Storefront Windows for You?

The storefront window business isn't for everyone. It takes a certain personality to compete and succeed at the storefront window business.

Good storefront window cleaners develop a sixth sense about new stores going into a shopping center. They instinctively watch for signs of life in the empty stores. Many times, not always though, the first window cleaner to reach the new storeowner gets the job. *The early window cleaner gets the job.*

2. Are you a salesperson?

Developing a storefront window cleaning business requires constant soliciting and takes a certain amount of courage going up to someone you don't know and asking them if their business needs a window cleaning service.

If you're not sure that you can go door-to-door, don't worry. Most people feel that way in the beginning. The trick is to persist and work past the negatives. If you feel after some rejection that you can't sell, there's another alternative: you can always buy another window cleaner's accounts. Some window cleaners get around the soliciting part by buying up small but profitable storefront routes and adding them to their already existing routes.

When you go out soliciting, though, be ready for the usual comments:

"No, we don't need a window cleaner,"
"We already have someone," or
"We do it ourselves."

After a while, most window cleaners develop a "thick skin" when soliciting, so that the selling part gets easier and sometimes fun. Sometimes getting a new storefront feels like new found money.

Finally, after many rejections, someone will ask those five words: "How much do you charge?"

Even then you will find opposition to your price, and then it happens. Someone finally says those magic words: "When can you start?"

3. Are you a competitor?

Storefront window cleaning is competitive, not just on price but selling ability and dogged perseverance. Do you have that drive to compete? If you played sports, you know that feeling of competing. The only difference is, instead of winning a game, you are winning a job. Sometimes winning the job feels like you have won a game.

4. Can you work for free?

Occasionally to get a job you need to throw in a few free extras to get the job started such as first cleanup is free, or you will clean up the construction mess —which can take up to five times longer — for the same monthly service price because you know in the long run you will make the money back and more, but it feels like you are working for free sometimes just to get the job. Years ago, depending on the competition, storefront window cleaners threw in all sorts of "freebies" just to get the job: six months free service, mirrors cleaned free every other month, or whatever little "clincher" that would get the job. Many window cleaners disagree with this philosophy and I'm not saying you must do this to be successful in the storefront business, but it can happen.

5. Are you more concerned about cleaning the window efficiently and quickly or about cleaning the window with care and perfection?

The majority of storeowners care more

about price than a perfect window. This doesn't mean you can get away with sloppy window cleaning, although some window cleaners do, but it does mean that to make money in storefront window cleaning, efficiency and speed play a major role. If you are the type of window cleaner that likes to take extra window cleaning care, look back and admire your work, or spend a few extra minutes inspecting the job for spots and lines or wipe the ledge and moldings for the third time, then storefront window cleaning may not be for you.

In storefront window cleaning you need to be able to clean a window, wipe the edges and give a quick glance for mistakes in cleaning and then move on to the next job. If you are the type that likes to take time on the job, then house window cleaning may be your ticket to success. Homeowners love to see a window cleaner take the time and care on their home. This does not mean you cannot be successful in the storefront business though.

6. Do you wash windows with about average speed?

As a general rule, storefront window cleaning is about speed and efficiency, not perfection and patience. When you are cleaning 50 + storefronts in a regular, efficient window cleaning day, then time is money. Those extra minutes you spend cleaning the job will add up by the end of the day. Speed means less time on each job which means more money earned per hour which means a bigger smile on your face.

7. Do you prefer using a ladder or pole?

Although using a ladder usually means cleaner windows, using an extension pole means saving time. Do you have a preference? Some window cleaners prefer using a ladder; it allows them closer access to the window in order to do the best job on the window. Other window cleaners prefer a pole which can clean just as well in many cases but also may leave streaks. Or, it can leave bars of dirt at the bottom of a high pane of glass where the ledge is too wide to squeegee all the way to the bottom of the window. For storefront windows, cleaning time is a factor and the majority of storefront window cleaners use a pole.

8. Do you mind socializing while you work?

Storefront owners like to talk, and the friendly conversation helps keep the business. The key, though, is to keep the socializing down to a minimum. The other point is that storefront owners come in a wide array of personalities during the day's work. Some window cleaners prefer working on hundreds of panes of glass without a soul in sight as in window cleaning in large office building complexes.

9. Do you prefer getting to a job and cleaning the entire day there or cleaning many different jobs and driving around?

Storefront window cleaning means cleaning for short periods of time and driving around to other stops on the route. Most window cleaners have a preference of either driving to many little shops or driving to one large house or building and spending the day. Which do you prefer?

10. Can you wait for your money? Can you play bill collector?

Storeowners can be notoriously slow payers either in person or through the mail. Jobs that pay cash mean when it is time to get paid the window cleaner takes the time to go to the cash register and sometimes wait five minutes or more for the money depending on the situation: customers, owner busy, or the owner is not there. Some storeowners will pay immediately, and they have the cash waiting for you. Most of the time this is the exception and not the rule.

If the payment is by check, then can you wait for your money? Most store owners will pay within the thirty days of receiving the bill; however, a good percentage (around 20 percent) of them will take their sweet time paying the bill. Corporate accounts are notoriously slow payers, some paying after 90 days.

Then there are the no paying customers. Can you play diplomatic bill collector, going back to the job over and over again trying to get your money or calling to see when you are going to receive a payment?

If you cannot wait for your money, then storefront window cleaning may not be for you. Homeowners almost always pay as soon as the job is completed.   Which do you prefer?

These are just a few questions that you should answer before jumping into the storefront business.

Variables when considering storefront window cleaning

Okay, you decided storefront window cleaning is for you. What next? Now look at what variables you need to notice when bidding store front window cleaning. Like house window cleaning, there are some questions to consider before building a storefront route.

Travel time to and from and between jobs?
What is blocking the window?
What signs or stickers are on the window?
How frequent the service?
Who is the competition?
What is the going rate per hour?

Travel Time

First, how far are you willing to travel to clean storefront windows? This depends on the type of storefront market you want to go after. Some window cleaners prefer to stay in one area.

For example, a window cleaner was offered a small 10-store route 50 minutes from his current area. He knew, though, that he wanted to stay in the county where he developed his business because the storefront market was open and growing. The work he was offered was in the next county, a place loaded with competitive window cleaners. He didn't want to fight to get work, so he declined the work though it was almost free. The work was not in his target market area, so he declined the offer.

Know your limits.

Driving to and from jobs, unloading and loading equipment, and washing the windows all takes time. The more spread out the window cleaning route the more time and money spent. The more stores a company cleans in a shopping center, the less they need to charge to make money. If driving time becomes a factor, some companies charge for that time or offer less service times per month.

What is blocking the window or on the window?

Like house windows, storefront windows can have objects blocking the windows or on the window. Moving objects out of your way and moving them back again eats away at precious time on the job. Will you have to move many things to get to the glass? Or, will the storeowner move them for you? Occasionally, storeowners will move the objects for you or move them back for you depending on what stipulations you set up with the storeowner. Some storeowners will move the items if you let them know when you are going to clean the inside windows. Other storeowners want you to do everything. How much work is involved in moving items?

What is on the window: Signs, Tint, and Security devices?

What's on the window is just as important as what's in front of the window. Signs, tints, and security devices can slow down the window cleaning process. Signs and posters taped to the window take time to remove. Sometimes you can work around the signs and other times you need to remove them. That leaves tape and tape marks on the glass that need to be scraped off. Stores that use lots of signs have lots of tape to be scraped. Signs can almost double the amount of time needed to clean the inside windows.

What some window cleaners do is suggest that the inside windows be cleaned every other month. Or, they make arrangements with the storeowner to remove the signs before the window cleaner does the windows. This sometimes works; in most cases, plan on removing the signs yourself. The door is cleaned inside each time.

In regions where the sun heats up the store's interior, storeowners will use window tint to protect store display items and lower the room temperature. Tint covering the inside windows generates another set of problems. The better the tint quality, the fewer window cleaning problems. Cheap tint,though, scratches easily and pulls away from the glass edges creating a dirty look to the window even when clean.

Frequency of Service

How often does the storeowner want his or her windows washed? Frequency of service becomes a factor in pricing. Usually, the more often the windows are cleaned, the less per cleaning a window cleaner charges per visit because the windows aren't as dirty.

Frequency of service can vary.

Weekly window cleaning may be the standard in some areas where competition is stiff and you have a high concentration of route work.

Twice a month, every two weeks or even once a month service is more common. Twice a month service means you arrive every first and third week of the month or every second and fourth week of the month. You can name what day of the week you think you will be there or just leave the service as first and third or second and fourth weeks of the month. Twice a month and once a month service works well for any type of route work, but it works especially well for those out of the way places or shopping centers where you have just a few accounts. Some window cleaners prefer to offer the every two weeks service. Since there is an average of 4.3 weeks in a month, some months will have five weeks in it. This is impor-

tant as some customers will ask if you are coming
every other week. You can do that, but then you
have to make a schedule that fits each store's
schedule. Every other week usually means more
work but also more headaches. Twice a month and
once a month service is usually a simpler approach
to setting up the routes.
Each has its advantages and disadvantages.

The advantage with weekly service is that it
allows a window cleaner to stay on top of his or
her route, keep an eye on business and competitors and stay in good communication with the store
owners. In areas of high competition, weekly service may be the way to go, so you can keep up a
good relationship with the storeowner. It's hard
for a competitor to take window work from a
friendly, reliable window cleaner that's at the store
once a week.

The disadvantage to weekly service is that
it doesn't allow for any flexibility in the route,
you're bound to that day of the week (yes,
storeowners will notice if you don't show up on
your scheduled day); also, your hourly rate may not
be as high as work cleaned twice a month.

The advantages to biweekly or twice a month
service is that it allows you some flexibility in the
route work. You don't have to show up on the same
day at the same time unless you set up the cleaning schedule that way. This way if a large job needs
to be done and you need to spend time on it, then
you have flexibility in moving your storefront route
off a day or two. Another advantage is that your
traveling time is cut in half.

Besides saving driving time, you can also
earn more per cleaning. For instance, many window cleaners that work a weekly job for $20 a

month could for that same job possibly earn $12 to $14 a month for twice a month service. (Note: these prices will vary and hopefully be higher than this example. Most customers will look at the bill and not the total number of cleanings.

The disadvantages of biweekly service are that you can't watch your work as often and the work is susceptible to competitor raiding. In this age of high vehicle expenses, more companies are turning to twice a month and monthly service.

Check out the competition

The competition for storefront windows is sharp. Sometimes three or four window cleaners or more compete for the same job, each trying to out do the other guy. Some towns have one window cleaner, but that one guy is so good at getting storefronts that no one else can compete. Competing in an area with many window cleaners with small routes is usually easier then competing against an established, experienced window cleaner. For a quick survey, go into stores and ask the owners who cleans the windows and how much they charge. You can honestly say you're not trying to get the window cleaning, you're just taking a survey.

If you hear the same company name at every store, then chances are good that the window cleaner in that area is highly competitive and would be tough to compete against in the long run. You may get some jobs in his territory; you might even be able to establish a route, but it's not going to be easy.

If you hear many different window cleaners' names and a wide array of prices, than the storefront market may be more open since the competition allows entry for so many window cleaners into the market.

In this case a faster way to develop a storefront route may be to buy out other smaller window cleaners. Many large storefront window cleaning companies not only solicit work but buy smaller routes to add to their own. Getting to know the other companies and offering to buy them out when they want to leave is a good way to increase business.

Look for the soft spot in the market place
A short coal mining story

An old coal miner watched a new kid mine for coal. The beginner walked over to a section of coal and began to chip away at the wall with a pickaxe. The coal broke off in little bits and pieces. After ten minutes of hard digging, the old coal miner could not bear to watch the kid working so hard for so little. He asked the young lad how the coal digging was going. The sweating, tired young man expressed his dismay at how much time and energy it took to get just a little bit of coal. The old man smiled and pointed to another wall farther down in the cavern and beckoned the young man to try there. The lad walked over and with one swing of the pickaxe pulled a large chunk of coal, more coal than he had been able to dig out in ten minutes from the other spot. He looked up astonished at the old timer who smiled back, "Find the soft spots in the coal and dig there."

If you'll pardon the metaphor, the same advice goes for storefront window cleaning: "Find the soft spot in the market and dig there."

The storefront market varies from town to town and from city block to city block. You never know what's available without first probing for the soft areas. In one town, the competition for storefront window cleaning may be fierce, and in the town just over the hill, the storefront business might be wide open with few or no window cleaners, or a window cleaner has stopped showing up or a window cleaner in the area gives poor service.

One window cleaner from Virginia moved to Southern California. The first thing he did was probe the markets around Southern California for areas of little or weak competition. He would go into an area, check the window ledges for dirt. (The window ledge gives you an idea how long it has been since the windows at that store had been cleaned. You can get pretty good at judging the degree of dust and dirt buildup.)

Then he spoke to the store owners about their window cleaning service: who was the window cleaner? How often did they service the windows and what did they charge? He would get some idea of window cleaning in that area. He would travel to the different cities of Southern California until he found an area where he felt he could build a storefront route.

Another good area to grow a route business is in cities and towns experiencing high growth rates. Economic booms and busts are constantly in motion all the time. While one city or county in one region of the country may be losing business because business enterprises had moved away or are feeling a slowdown, another city or county in another region of the country may be experiencing a rapid growth rate with shopping malls are going up all over the place. A case in point would be Las Vegas, Nevada. At one time 10,000 new people per month were moving to the area. That meant new shopping centers to take care of the new residents.

A word about "stealing" work

Going in and underbidding another window cleaner's job just to get work is called "stealing" work. Here's what happens. You go and take a job from another window cleaner. You say you can do the job for half the other guy's rate. Now, you have to work for half as much. Maybe you can, but why would you? The other thing that happens is the window cleaner who lost the job will find out who is taking his or her work and somewhere in the future, he'll try and do the same thing to you. What happens in the long run is both window cleaners lose. Both work for a price below their expectations. This in turn causes one or both window cleaners to begin to take shortcuts on the job: clean only the lower half of the window (called haircutting the job), skip cleanings, rush through the job, or any number of creative, get-out-of-work options. In short, trying to underbid a job from a window cleaner that's already providing a good service at reasonable prices hurts everyone in the long run.

Getting work from a window cleaner who is not showing up, does poor work, or displays less than a business-like manner is a different story. The free enterprise system is alive and well as it should be. Allowing poor window cleaning business practices to continue is also unacceptable. You get into trouble in the long run when you low bid your storefront jobs

In the beginning, new window cleaners have a tendency to underbid the job in order to get business. In the short run, this theory works. You feel satisfied. You're working; you're making money, not great money, but it's something. Then you start to develop a pattern of bidding low to get the job. Sure you can do the work for less money;

it's only labor. You might even feel proud to be able to offer services for such a price.

The problems arise in the long run. You might begin to feel the pinch of working for such a low sum; when this happens you might start cutting corners on the job, not doing all the windows or cleaning the windows too quickly and leaving mistakes. At the end of the year, you won't have enough money to pay taxes or maybe you noticed it by the time quarterly taxes are due.

Where you really begin to feel the pinch is when you want to hire a worker. How much can you really pay them? You haven't got enough profit built into your price to pay anyone. Or, you hire someone but don't pay workman's compensation or take out the proper taxes.

A number of window cleaners go out of business because they underpriced their work, and in the long run, it killed them.

Getting a feel for what a customer will pay

Finally, a word about your gut feeling — with experience some window cleaners develop a sixth sense as to what a storeowner will pay and how long the job will take. He can go in to the storeowner knowing the type of business and what those jobs will pay.

For example, donut shops usually don't pay well while doctor's offices usually do.

The object in business is to make money. Occasionally, though, you take a lower price on a job to keep another window cleaner out, but then be able to get the price you need later at another job.

These are just a few points to ponder before you get into the storefront window cleaning business.

STOREFRONT WINDOW CLEANING

Chapter 9

BIDDING STOREFRONT WINDOWS

In this chapter you will find all the bidding methods possible for storefront windows. In addition, a few of the extra tasks asked of window cleaners will be covered also. These extras include holiday paint and spray snow removal.

Minimum Charge

Many window cleaners prefer to use a minimum charge per job no matter what type of window cleaning. Storefront window cleaning is no different. Storefront window cleaning minimums are lowest when compared to all other types of window cleaning. Minimum pricing varies from window cleaner to window cleaner. Some window cleaners don't mind cleaning for $10 minimum per job while other window cleaners would not touch a job that's less than $15 or higher. You need to decide ahead of time what is the minimum you would charge to stop and clean a store.

With the minimum price established, now look at the different ways of bidding storefront windows. As with house window cleaning, there are a number of ways to bid.

By market pricing
By the hour
By the store
By the pane
By the square foot
By cross reference

Market Pricing

Since storefront window cleaning is so competitive in most areas, the market pricing approach keeps you even with the competition. If you are new to the window cleaning business, then market pricing will help you be competitive quickly in the competitive market.

In market pricing a window cleaner attempts to stay competitive by knowing the going rate for other window cleaning in the area.

The first way to use market pricing is conduct a survey of the storeowners in the area where you want to develop a route. You ask the store owners in that given area, what their window cleaner charges for the window cleaning, how often the window cleaner comes by: weekly? biweekly? or monthly? In market pricing survey, you're just trying to gather information about what the competition is charging, how many competitors are in the area, and who they are, so that when you bid new stores going into a shopping center or find a store that doesn't have a window cleaner, then you will know the going rates for service and be able to stay competitive, although you can go higher.

Sometimes the storeowner doesn't remember how often the windows are cleaned and will guess at the service. Sometimes they will flat-out lie, but the majority of storeowners will give you an honest answer. To be on the safe side, just ignore the highest price and the lowest price for similar jobs; the middle pricing will get you close to the going rates.

After a while, with practice, a good window cleaner can look at a job and know at what price range a new store's window cleaning would fall and the needs of that store in that area.

The second way to use market pricing is in a direct approach to your storefront bidding. When you go in to bid a store that's looking for a window cleaner, you ask if the owner has received any bids yet and if so, what are the bids?
You would be surprised how many storeowners will gladly tell you the current bids, so you know who and what you're up against, and you start your pricing from there. Maybe you can meet the current bid and sell the owner on your service. Maybe you clean all the other stores in the shopping center, and you're at that shopping center all the time. Store owners like to hire a window cleaner that is the "window cleaner for the center." They put that thought in their mind when choosing a window cleaner. The fact that you already clean other stores in the center is a plus. Maybe you can ex-

plain your expertise in cleaning the windows of his or her particular store. You offer suggestions for the type of service and why. Maybe the inside windows will need cleaning every week because of the type of store.

Sometimes the other bids are high and you can actually make good money with a lower bid. Maybe everyone else offers weekly service, but you offer biweekly service at a lower rate. There are all sorts of options to getting the job.

One window cleaner became skilled at cleaning the moldings so well they looked brand new when he finished cleaning. He developed his route work by offering to polish up the moldings as well. He went the other way from the competition. While everyone else was trying to get the price lower and doing cheaper work, he stayed at the higher end of the bidding offering the highest quality of service. He didn't go for volume but for price and quality. This method worked for him to an extent.

The third way to use market pricing is to approach the potential customers and ask them how much they want to spend on the window cleaning. (Don't laugh, it works sometimes.) The storeowner may have an amount in mind that he or she wants to spend on the window cleaning. With that price in mind, you know what work you can do for that price.

Bidding by the hour

Whether it's once a month, twice a month, or weekly service, you can estimate how many hours it will take to clean the job and multiply that number by the hourly rate you want to earn. For the large window cleaning jobs like restaurants, this method works well.

Don't be afraid to make money.

Most storefront window cleaners earn on the average of $50 per hour (as of this printing) and that includes the driving time.

Some window cleaners will take a daily rate and average all the jobs together. At the end of the day, they calculate how many hours they were away from home and how much money they earned in that time period.

If the rate is less than expected, then they may look to raise the price for service for any new jobs on the route. Or, they may ask existing customers for a price increase. Either way, they want to increase what they make an hour.

Occasionally, a window cleaner attempts to earn a certain hourly rate, but the window cleaner is slow and takes too long to clean windows. Because he is using the hourly rate to set his prices and he is so slow, his rate is three times what the competition charges. He might be able to get that price for a while, but if he is too far above what the competition is charging for the job, then eventually, he will lose those jobs. That type of window cleaner may better serve the homeowner market. Storeowners are extremely price conscious. Any prices well above what is normal for the area usually doesn't last long. Be within reason if you're bidding by the hour.

Bidding by the store

A popular trend in window cleaning is acquiring chain store accounts. A chain of stores wants one company to clean all their stores. Some

window cleaners will bid the job by the store offering one price for each store in an effort to
sweeten the offer. Some chain store accounts are
a "cookie cutter" of each other, so it's easy to give
just one price. Some stores may vary in size and
number of windows, but the window cleaner gives
an average price figuring that whatever time he
loses on the larger stores, he will make up the difference on the smaller jobs. Individual store pricing is also an option. The key is that the company
only needs to write one check.

Bidding by the window pane

Bidding by the pane is an accurate method,
but not always a competitive one. Nonetheless it does
give you a base price from which to work from.
You calculate the price based upon a standard 4'
by 8' plate of glass or by sections of glass that seem
standard to your shopping centers. In California
many new retail store window sections have two
windows, a long window over a small window or
reversed, small window over a long window. The
window styles have more to do with safety than
decorative window architecture. You can decide for
yourself how you want to set the price if you wish
to bid by window section or by window pane. See
samples one, two and three on how the pricing
works.

In reality, there is an average of 4.3 weeks
in each month. That means sometimes there will
be five weeks in the month. Are you going

Example One: Once a month cleaning

For example, if you have chosen the base price of cleaning one side of a 4 by 8 pane of glass a dollar per side, then the price for one time service inside and outside would look as follows. Note: the $1 per side is used in the sample for simplicity's sake; the actual price per pane will vary with each region.

For example:
A clothing store you are going to bid has two 4-foot by 8-foot glass panels and a door. If you're bidding the job for once a month inside and outside, the calculations would look like this.

W = window   D = door

Price for once a month service, inside and outside

	W	W	D
Outside	$1	$1	$1
Inside	$1	$1	$1
Total	$2	+ $2	+ $2 = $6

Note: If that price is below your minimum charge, then your minimum charge would become your bid price.

Example Two

If that same job was twice a month outside and once a month inside and the door is cleaned in and out each time, then the price would look like this:

Price for twice a month service.

	W	W	D
Outside $2	$2	$2	
Inside	$1	$1	$2
Total	$3	$3 +	$4 = $10 per month

Example Three

If the job was to be weekly, a standard window cleaning service would be what's called a four and one service, four times outside and one time inside with the door in and out each time.

Price for weekly service

	W	W	D
Outside $4	$4	$4*	
Inside	$1	$1	$4*
Total	$5 +	$5 +	$8 = $18 a month

*Inside door is cleaned weekly

to charge for that time? How will you handle that extra week in the month?

A per pane pricing is a good starting point for the bid. If the job is one that has objects in front of the windows or the windows are filled with grease and fingerprints, then you may want to adjust your bid upwards. If the competition is stiff and the job is important to the business, then you may wish to adjust the price downward.

Study the competition

If you want to find out what the competitors are charging per pane then ask the customers and then divide the number of panes cleaned in a month by the amount charged. Chances are good that the price per pane will fluctuate from job to job, but that an overall average price per pane should begin to emerge after a while.

For example, you walk into a store and find out the competitor is charging $15 a month for twice a month service for two large window panes and two doors: the windows are cleaned twice outside, once inside a month and the two doors are in and out each time. This is a standard twice a month cleaning as of this printing.

Now, do the math. The two large panes receive six cleanings a month [two outsides twice that's 4 times and the inside sides once (2) for a total of six times. The two doors are cleaned in and out for a total of 8 times. The total number of sides cleaned is 14 (8 +6 =14)]. If the window cleaner receives $15 per month, then the price charged per pane is $1.07 per side.

Bidding by the square foot

With the modern look of odd size panes or extra large panes, some window cleaners utilize a price per square foot of glass. Although this bidding method has been used by the janitorial industry for years when bidding floors, the window cleaning industry is just beginning to experiment with a square foot price.

In Japan, some window cleaning companies use a per square foot of glass price in their bidding. At one time, five cents per square foot was the average rate.

Example of square foot pricing

Example: One store front with a 12-foot by 12-foot pane of glass and one door to be cleaned inside and outside.

One 12-foot by 12-foot window (both sides)
    inside   12 x 12 = 144 square feet
    outside 12 x 12 = 144 square feet
        Total   =   288 square feet

One door (both sides)
    inside   3 x 7   = 21 square feet
    ouside   3 x 7   = 21 square feet
        Total   =   42 square feet

Window square footage =   288
Door square footage   =   42
Total window surface area   =   330 square feet
Take 330 square feet and mulitiply it by five cents you get the following: 330 square feet x 5-cents = $16.50 bid price. So, your starting point on bidding would be around $16.50. Then make any adjustments you feel are necessary.

Using your gut feeling

With new shopping centers using the same type of windows to give the center a uniform look, after a while, you can develop a "gut feeling" for a fair and competitive price in a shopping center.

When you bid enough storefront windows, you get a feel for what the actual price could be for just about any storefront job. You can tell when someone underbids the job.

You can also tell when someone has overbid the job, charging three or four times the going rate for window cleaning.

Think about the storeowner's point of view. Imagine that you take your window cleaning vehicle to get an oil change and the place charges $150 just to change the oil. Do you think that business would be around long? Probably not. The storefront window business is similar. If a window cleaner comes in and bids $65 a month for cleaning two windows and a door once a week, that window cleaner will not be around long because the free market price system will eventually bring enough competitors through that store, and the storeowner will realize he's paying way too much for service.

There's a difference between getting top dollar for the work you perform and overcharging for that same work.

With experience you get a feel for the different types of storefront pricing: underbidding, competitive pricing, high end pricing, and over charging. The competitive and high end pricing (upmarket pricing) work is more a function of how much a storeowner can and will pay for the service. The upmarket price also gives you some flexibility to offer your customer a discount when one is appropriate.

You also will get a feel for what types of stores are willing to pay a high end price or up-market price and which stores will seek out the lowest, bottom market price. For example, donut shops are notorious for not wanting to pay much for service and dentist offices usually don't mind paying a high end, upmarket price. Within minutes of talking with the storeowner, you can sometimes get a feel for what the owner will pay.

The Bottom Feeders

Some window cleaners will only use rockbottom pricing for the service when competition shows up. Their price is half or less of the competitors because they want to chase the competition away, keeping them from getting any work in a center. New window cleaners can do this for a little while, but then the hidden costs mentioned earlier begin to catch up with them: insurance, taxes, car depreciation, etc.

The larger window cleaning companies can afford to use this technique for two reasons: first they usually have hundreds of storefront accounts, sometimes thousands of storefront accounts. These companies can actually clean the new jobs for free if necessary to get the job because they make excellent money on most of their other accounts. Their profit is in their other well established accounts. These accounts are in areas where the competition is less a factor, and the window cleaner can charge a more high end price or upmarket price. By keeping out competitors in the beginning, these window cleaners set themselves up to be able to charge more later on when the competition becomes less a factor.

Storeowners want value

The object in business is to make money, but at the same time the storeowners must perceive that they are receiving a good value for their dollar. Most window cleaners cannot afford to match a large window company's low end pricing but there are ways to stay competitive.

One way to compete in bidding

One way of competing with companies that offer weekly service for cheap is to offer twice a month or once a month service for the same price or slightly discounted price. Surprisingly, many storeowners don't mind you servicing them just twice a month or once a month to save a few dollars; many times that's all the store needs anyway. As an extra incentive for the store owner that's worried about major spills on their windows and you're not due for another week, offer to come out for any emergency clean up that might arise for free. You might get a call from that customer once every few years to come out and clean up a spill.

Cross Referencing

Cross referencing means to compare one method of bidding with another in order to compare two ways of pricing. Many window cleaners will use this combination for cross checking the bid prices. Cross referencing can give the window cleaner some idea of the storefront market in that area. For instance, let's say that you walk into a store with windows that haven't been cleaned in a long time. You find out that the owner had a window cleaner, but that the old window cleaner stopped showing up. He wants you to bid the windows.

If you count the number of panes and find a price per pane, then do a market approach (maybe ask the store owner what the old window cleaner charged) you find that the absent window cleaner's price was half the per pane price you charge. In essence it looked like the other window cleaner had underbid the job, felt disillusioned with the work and stopped coming or found better work or acquired so much work he can't do all the jobs anymore and stopped showing up (that happens also).

With both prices — per pane price and market approach price — you get a general idea about the job. With the per pane price, you can show the storeowner that the other window cleaner's price was well below what was normal for the area and that you can clean the windows based more on the per pane price.

Another way you can use the cross reference approach is with hard to gauge stores. Many experienced and inexperienced window cleaners really get a feel for what to charge on a new account. Occasionally, that gut feeling of what to charge just doesn't happen or a price comes to you but you just don't feel comfortable with that price. So, occasionally, when your gut feeling of a price doesn't feel right, you might do some cross referencing and check your gut feeling price with another method of bidding, maybe the market approach or per pane pricing. You just need to compare the price to another bidding method to feel more comfortable with the price.

Bidding paint or snow removal

Stores paint advertising signs on the windows to increase sales or promote the holiday season. The painted areas will vary. Maybe they paint a small section or the entire window. Sometimes the store likes to keep the sign up all year, and sometimes they'll keep it up just two weeks. Whenever the time comes to replace the sign, you'll be asked to remove the paint from the glass.

Like construction cleanups, paint removal can be easy or a nightmare. With practice, though, any window cleaner can become proficient at the bidding and paint removal.

Paint removal on storefront windows is a mixed blessing, and window cleaners can approach the paint removal bidding process a few different ways. If the storefront owner is not a regular customer, then the bid price should reflect that. Usually, a price of up to five times the regular window cleaning price or higher depending on the type of paint and how many windows, should be applied. Some window cleaners charge a flat five dollars or more per plate or window for paint removal.

Others will bid the job judging how long the job will take them. Remember the windows will need to be washed, scraped, washed, and squeegeed and that's assuming you will be able to get all the paint off on the first try which is highly unlikely which means you would have to wet and scrape and squeegee the windows a few times. This all takes time, so figure at least three times the normal window cleaning. So, if a job takes you a half-hour to clean, then figure an hour and a half for the cleaning and paint removal and multiply that time by your hourly rate. The cleaning time will depend on the number of windows painted and the area of glass painted, but this should give you a rough estimate to start.

If the customer is a regular job that goes at least once a month, then there are two other possibilities.

The first choice is that you don't charge for the paint removal. That's right. When store windows are cleaned weekly or twice a month, then there is a time period when the window cleaner cannot clean the windows because of the paint. This happens usually around the holiday season in December. Since the windows can't be cleaned and the window cleaner still desires that regular paycheck at the end of the month, many window cleaners will strike a deal with the storeowner to remove the holiday paint for the same price as charged for the window service per month. So, when the window cleaner just cleans the door because the windows are painted, he saves time and that time, in essence, is banked for the time when he has to clean off the paint. Most storeowners will accept the idea, but a small percentage of them will argue that you didn't have to clean the windows for the month because of the paint.

That's when you can bring up the other possibility: you do charge for the paint removal. The paint removal will take roughly as long as you would have spent cleaning the windows if the job were cleaned weekly and sometimes longer. So, figure accordingly. Sometimes window cleaners will apply a surcharge to the window cleaning monthly price, usually something nominal that's added to the monthly price. This may depend upon what the competition is doing and your own needs. Again, don't be afraid to make money.

"In fifty years, no one will care or even remember who cleaned the windows on a building, but the memory of how one was treated by a competitor will linger for a life-time."

The Wise Window Cleaner

Chapter 10

MID-RISE WINDOW CLEANING

Some of the most lucrative jobs in window cleaning today include the mid-rise window cleaning market. These jobs don't get the attention received by houses, storefronts, and high-rise window cleaning.

The mid-rise window cleaning market includes all buildings from one to three stories. These are the buildings that can still be cleaned from the ground up instead of from the top of the building down.

Most window cleaners, happily cleaning houses or storefront windows, usually feel a bit awestruck and perplexed at attempting to bid these jobs or clean them. They started their business cleaning houses or storefront windows and don't want to come out of their comfort zone of what

they know. After all, these jobs require extra
equipment, more insurance, and lots of labor and
stamina. The high-rise window cleaning companies would gladly clean mid-rise windows and do,
but for some companies their money and their
time is invested in the bigger jobs, so they can't
spend the time or money soliciting all the one or
two building jobs.

Maybe a janitorial company that cleans the
offices is responsible for cleaning the outside windows, and they contract with someone to clean
windows. Usually a janitorial company pays the
minimum price possible to get the windows
cleaned. Larger high-rise companies usually can't
afford to clean windows for that cheap a price.
They have costs that will not allow it.

So the combination of forces, smaller window cleaning companies not willing to change and
larger companies not able to grab all the market,
leaves a mid-rise market that can be lucrative.

A few mid-rise buildings can and should be
cleaned using a stage or boatswain's chair, but for
this chapter we'll concentrate on bidding practices
that bid the job for cleaning from the ground using either a ladder, a boom-lift, an extension pole,
or a water-fed pole.

If you're cleaning a building using the chair
or stage from the roof, then move on to the chapter on high-rise window cleaning.

Are mid-rise window cleaning jobs for you?

The process of bidding and cleaning mid-
rise or high-rise windows differs from bidding
houses and storefronts. Before you start in mid-
rise window cleaning, there are a few things you
should know before going into this type of work.

MID-RISE WINDOW CLEANING

1. Cleaning windows on mid-rise buildings usually will require insurance and proof of insurance.

Most window cleaners that clean houses and storefronts do not carry window cleaning insurance. Insurance, however, is a necessary step for window cleaners who want to move into the mid-rise business.

While some building or business owners will not ask for your insurance, the majority of those in charge of the mid-rise buildings will. Even a few janitorial companies may not ask for a copy of your insurance, assuming that their insurance will cover the window cleaning, but beware, most janitorial insurance policies *do not* cover window cleaning and will state that fact in their policy. So, if you are serious about getting into the mid-rise window cleaning business, then research where to find window cleaning insurance, ask companies where they buy their window cleaning insurance or check with the IWCA.

2. Cleaning windows on mid-rise buildings usually requires an investment in more equipment and labor.

To clean mid-rise buildings, depending on the building, you might need to purchase other equipment: Ladders, extension poles, or a water-fed pole. Maybe you need to rent a boom-lift to reach the windows. Using the new equipment requires training and practice. Large buildings such as these can require more than one person to complete the cleaning.

3. Be prepared to clean one window after another, after another with no person in sight.

145

There are no breaks in mid-rise window cleaning. Unlike house windows and storefronts where after a few hours you're on to the next job, or you are cleaning a variety of windows, mid-rise window cleaning is row after row of the same windows until the job is completed —and the job could take days. Some window cleaners prefer that monotony while others prefer a break in the service: driving, talking to customers, other sights and sounds.

Checklist for mid-rise window cleaning

The bidding process for mid-rise windows begins with gathering data. By taking this extra time to collect as much information about the building or buildings, you save yourself the grief of missing valuable information while you put together the bid for your potential customer.

Most established mid-rise and even high-rise window cleaners create a worksheet with all the questions they need to answer. This is important to the bidding process. Not that you can't walk around the building and get a good feel for what price you want for the job. You can; however, by putting together a Bid Information Sheet, save yourself possible grief and wasted time.

A Bid Information Sheet lists all the questions for which you need answers in order to bid the building. By answering these questions you create a professional image for your company.

The following questions should be on your Bid Information Sheet.

Who is the contact person for the building?

The old adage, "You never get a second

chance to make a first impression" holds true for soliciting and bidding window cleaning accounts. Introduce yourself, make eye contact, thank him or her for the opportunity to bid the window cleaning, hand the person a business card, ask for a business card.

Are there any brochures, pamphlets, or copies of the building or business park layout?

As you discuss the window cleaning needs of the building, ask if there are any diagrams of the building, buildings, or business park. This is especially nice when the windows may have certain cleaning challenges. Also, a diagram or layout helps you visualize the work ahead. You can make notes about water outlets, areas with obstacles, and best place to set up equipment.

What service is required and how often?

Window cleaning needs vary. How often will the building exterior be cleaned in a year? Once? Twice? Quarterly? Monthly? Is it just a one time cleaning? How often will the inside windows be cleaned? Some office buildings require a monthly service to keep certain windows always clean.

Besides clean windows, what are the concerns of the building manager or owner?

Does he or she wish a bid on calcium removal?

What is the layout of the building?

Here you need to know what the building looks like from the top and side views. Sketching the outline of the building looking down on it, you get a grasp of how many sides and how many windows on each side and each floor. This information can be written next to the drawing. You can sketch the building as big or small as you like; whatever works for you.

Before you count the windows though, you need the most important information of all.

Where's the water?

Before you do anything else, find out about the water supply. Go around the building and find all the water outlets. If you can't find them or you think there are more then you have found, then go find someone that knows. Groundskeepers usually know where the water is located. Mark an "X" on your drawing everywhere that water is located. Getting to the water to clean the windows can be a major problem in mid-rise window cleaning. Where you are cleaning the windows and where the water is located may be 500 yards apart. If you are using a water-fed pole, then you need to calculate the number of hoses necessary to clean the building(s).

What type of water key is needed?

Getting access to the water may also be a problem. Nothing is more frustating than going out to clean the windows on an office building, getting the equipment all set up and forgetting the specific water key necessary to turn on the water or not having the proper water key to turn on the water. Always find out what type of water-key is required to turn on the water. Bring more than one water key or a pair of pliers.

Sometimes the water is located on the building wall and a simple water key is all it takes to turn on the water. Sometimes the water is locked behind a panel or in the ground. A water spigot in the ground requires a special water key or keys. Write down what type of water key is necessary to turn on the water.

What are the window sizes and shapes?

Look at the size and shape of the windows. Usually the windows on a mid-rise building come in one to four different shapes and sizes. On some buildings, all the windows are exactly the same all the way around the building. Other buildings have various sizes, but usually no more than four different shapes or sizes.

On the bid sheet, sketch out the different window shapes and sizes.

Write down the length and width of each window. For each window shape, assign it a letter. You may bid all the windows the same price, but at least you get some idea of size and shape. You can never have too much information for the bidding process. Most mid-rise buildings have four or less window sizes.

Do the windows open?

If you are cleaning sliding or double-hung windows, then chances are you cannot use a water fed pole system. Well sealed stationary windows are the best windows for using that system.

Does the building have only windows or is the entire building covered with windows and spandrels?

Glass used for the design of the building and not as windows are called spandrels. On some buildings the entire exterior is covered with windows and spandrels, and you can't tell the difference between the two unless you get right up to the glass or the lights in the offices are turned on at night. Count all the glass on the building; it all must be cleaned even if it can't be seen through; the overall appearance of the building depends on it.

How many windows on each floor?

Count the number of windows on each floor, the window size and what side of the building the windows face. (Some buildings have sides with no windows. Knowing these sides helps you plan the window cleaning as well as refresh your memory when you look back at the building data.)

What is the composition of the exterior?

Some buildings are all glass exteriors which means using an extension pole or water fed pole for cleaning. Occasionally an extension ladder or stack ladder can by used on certain structural elements such as moldings. Ladders placed against windows can and will crack the window no matter how lightly you think the ladder leans against the glass. Putting the ladder closer to the building may take much of the pressure off the ladder ends, but you sacrifice safety to clean the windows. Remember, safety first, cleaning second.

The building exterior is important. The consistency of the wall can alter how you clean the windows or what equipment you will need.

For example, if the exterior is smooth white painted concrete, then drips and runs from the window cleaning will show up on the wall if you use squeegees and extension poles and if the drips are left on the wall, the drips will stain and discolor the wall.

Cleaning off the dirt drips from the wall below the windows takes time. If the drip marks are left to dry, they may permanently mark the wall. A squeegee and scrubber system may work for the cleaning but extra time may be needed to wipe the wall and to remove drips.

If you use a water fed pole, then all the dirt is flushed from the building wall and drips are not a problem. If a squeegee and scrubber are used to clean the windows, then a scrubber (wand) is used to wipe the wall.

Ladder marks can also pose a problem. Ladder ends left uncovered leave unsightly marks and scuffs. It's a sick feeling to do a great job on the window cleaning but stand back and see dark scuff marks left on the wall.

Rough sandblasted concrete walls will not show stains and you don't have to spend time wiping the walls or worrying about ladder marks.

Are there any cracks, scratches, stains, or damaged windows?

As you walk around the building keep your eyes open for any cracked or scratched windows. If you think something seems unusual about a window, go up close, inspect it from the sides and with the sun directly on the plate (remember that the sun shows all the abnormalities of a window). Look for any cracks or scratches and write them down on your bid information sheet. By noting and reporting all cracks, stains, and damaged windows, you save yourself a lot of grief later trying to explain to the person in charge that you did not cause the damage.

Cracks can be caused any number of ways. Sometimes the building shifts and extra pressure

151

on the glass causes it to crack. Sometimes the former window cleaner cracked the window (cold water from a water fed pole on hot glass can crack the glass; so can a ladder leaned against a window).

Scratched glass is most common and the hardest to spot through dirty windows. Look at the glass with the sun reflecting on it. Go up to any window where you see any unusual reflection that highlights fine lines etched in the glass.

Acid burns and weakened window protection are less common than scratched glass but still a concern. Acid burns and weakened window protection are caused by either using the wrong acids on the windows to remove calcium deposits or using the acids too often on the windows which will cause a breakdown of the smooth surface area on the glass. The acid burns appear milky white on dark colored glass and a foggy look on clear or slightly tinted windows, a reaction with the glass surface. Mirrored windows, when burned by acid, look discolored with the mirrored element of the window destroyed and a dark discoloration appears.

Look at the windows carefully. You are about to be held responsible for the windows when you get the job.

Are there any calcium deposits or other stains on the glass?

Note any calcium deposits on the glass. Calcium deposits form when hard water from the sprinkers dry on the glass repeatedly. Let the property managers know before you clean that the calcium deposits are not part of your regular window cleaning, but a separate service. Or, you can make the calcium deposit removal part of the bid price if requested.

Another problem is lime stains. Lime stains are caused by poor sealing of the concrete walls; rain leaches lime out of the concrete and deposits it on the window. Here again, write down notations about windows with these problems. Lime stains appear as a stain coming down from the top portion of the window. Sometimes the stain looks like water lines of deposits running down the glass, and other times it looks like a light curtain of stain on the glass. These deposits will not come off with regular window cleaning. Mention to the person in charge that the building or buildings may have lime stains (sometimes you can't tell until you wash the window) that will not come off with window cleaning. The owner or manager may already know about the poor sealing of the building.

Are the windows flush with the wall or are they set in from the wall?

Windows flush with the wall

Windows flush with the wall are the easiest to clean. You don't need to worry about squeegeeing the water to the bottom of the window. There are no barriers.

Windows with two-inch moldings

Windows with two-inch moldings and the glass set in from the wall present a problem, but new innovations in window cleaning equipment and adjusting your style of cleaning can usually get around this.

Windows set in from the wall

Windows set in farther from the wall present a problem; the way the windows are cleaned may need to be devised or created. Maybe just ladders can by used although you have to climb up to every window. Maybe a boom-lift must be rented to get to the windows. Maybe water-fed pole extensions are required to reach the windows. Windows set in from the wall take more time to clean.

What do the ground and landscape look like?

Land that slopes away from the building puts the windows farther away. You may think that all your poles and ladders will reach the windows, but ground that drops away from the building can make a normal two-story building seem four stories high. Also sloping ground means unlevel areas for a ladder. What will you use to secure the ladder base on solid equal footing? Check the ground around the building.

Are there any obstacles? Trees?

Trees are probably the greatest hindrance to window cleaning. Getting around them or through them to get to the windows takes extra time. Some windows may be impossible to clean because tree branches press against the windows. Again, let the property manager know the situation with the trees.

Where are the cars parked?

Cars also pose a problem. Parking lots are designed with spaces that go up to the building wall. Moving in and around and over cars worth more than $50,000 would make any window cleaner nervous and makes for a hazardous working condition. Two things need to be decided:

First, are you going to ask the owner or property manager to tell people to park their cars away from that window cleaning zone? Or, are you going to clean the windows early in the morning or late at night or on the weekend? Even on the weekend, you will probably find cars parked under the windows.

How high up the wall are the windows?

Again, nothing can be more frustating than driving to the building site with a ladder or pole that will not reach the windows. To avoid this, calculate the highest point you have to reach to clean. Most floors on a commercial building average 12 feet per floor, so your first "guesstimate" might be 12 feet, 24 feet, and 36 feet to the top of that floor, but conditions on and around the building may make the windows higher than you think, or the building may have a parapet wall that extends the glass cleaning above the top floor.

Three ways to check the building height:
1. Carry your equipment with you.

Many times you just want to know if your poles or ladders will reach the highest point on the glass. Before you bid a job, make sure you have your longest extension pole in your vehicle. That way if your mind tells you that the building height may be too high for your equipment, or you just want to check to make sure the equipment will reach, then pull-out the extension pole, go to the highest point on the glass and pretend you're attempting to squeegee the window. This way you know that equipment will reach and you have the right size pole.

2. Estimate the size of the building.

Estimate the window's vertical dimension on the first floor, if the windows on the upper floors are the same, then estimate the area distance between the first floor and second floor. Once you have the first floor height (window height + wall height) then double it to get the height of a two-story building and triple it to get the height of a three-story building. Usually twelve feet per floor is a good estimate to begin with, but are the windows near the top or bottom of that twelve feet per floor? It makes a big difference.

3. Estimate the height using your equipment.

Even if you only carry a two-section extension pole, by holding the pole up to the building you can "ballpark" the height.

What other obstacles are in the way?

Look around the building; imagine yourself cleaning the windows; plan every move you might make to clean the glass. Now, what might interfere with your cleaning?

Remember safety first.

Some examples of obstacles you might find as you visualize the window cleaning process on the building might be the following:

Powerlines: How close are the powerlines to the building? Using a water fed pole system is highly dangerous around power lines.

Other electrical facilities: Using ladders and water are a lousy combination around power facilities. (One window cleaner's employee using a water nozzle sprayed an electrical outlet that caught fire. Another company using water around a large lighted sign short-circuited the lighting)

Heavily used walkways: When and where will people that work in the building enter and exit the building? Knowing the high traffic times and high traffic areas can help you plan when to clean those areas if the cleaning is on a work day or when the business is open. What adjustments will you have to make? Will you need barriers, caution signs, or another worker to help with safety maintenance?

Walls, fences, or locked gates: Whether you're pulling hoses or carrying a ladder, walls, fences or locked gates will cause you to detour or reset your equipment. In the case of a locked gate, will someone unlock it for you? When?

Obstacles on the building: What canopies, iron bars, and decorative objects will obstruct window cleaning? Window canopies make ladder work difficult. Can you still reach upper story windows with the canopy in the way? Upper story windows with iron bars present other challenges. Some bars are set far enough away from the window to allow an extension pole access to the window while others are set close to the window so that they can only be cleaned by using a ladder to reach them for cleaning.

Boom-lift obstacles: If you plan to use a boom-lift, imagine moving around the building. Can you get close enough to the building from all areas around the building? Is the ground firm enough to support the boom-lift?

Which way does the sun cross the sky in relationship to the buildings?

This may sound like a funny question to ask yourself, but it pays big dividends later when planning out the window cleaning. Most window cleaners do not want to work in direct sunlight, because water evaporates quickly on hot glass, and cold water from the water fed poles can crack hot glass. So on paper sketch the path of the sun and draw an arrow marking which way is North. Southern exposed glass in the United States gets the most sun while the East side gets blasted in the morning and the West side in the afternoon. By figuring out the path of the sun, you can plan out which side of the building to begin on or the best time to clean the windows.

Window cleaners can work in the sun, but heat and sunlight sap vital energy and expose workers to possible skin cancer conditions.

What unusual window placements or building designs make cleaning more difficult?

Draw out any unusual window architecture that may cause you cleaning problems. For instance, slanted sunroofs over the foyer or walkways with glass roofs or windows set deep from the building wall or windows that make your mind scream *warning*, these are window areas where you need to devise a safe way of cleaning them.

Building entrances have grandiose looking appearances with many windows. A well-cleaned entrance sets the tone for the cleanliness of the building. By spending a little extra time making sure the entrance windows and moldings are cleaned well, you set the tone that the building is clean.

By sketching out these problem areas, you can study them back at your office or use them later to help your employees understand some of the challenges of the building.

What about the inside window cleaning?

If you're bidding the inside windows too, then walk the inside inspecting and counting windows. Unlike the exterior where window cleaning is usually easily accessed with one window after another, interior windows usually have walls, desks, plants, doors, and other barriers and detours. Interior windows can take up to fifty percent longer to complete because of these objects, plus working around the tenant's own schedule. Before you bid the inside windows, be able to answer these questions.

Is the inside foyer two-story or higher?

Inside foyers can be two stories high and higher. Most inside foyer windows sit in deep three or four inch moldings. Using an extension pole becomes nearly impossible because you can't get the squeegee far enough down the glass to clean a window, so ladders will be needed. Again estimate the height of the highest point of glass needed to be cleaned. Most inside foyers can be reached with a 24-foot or 28-foot ladder, but on rare occasions the foyer will be 30 to 36 feet high and a 40-foot ladder will be necessary.

Are there stairs in the way?

If stairs are a problem, then ladder levelers or some type of leveling device will be needed to set up a ladder.

Does the foyer have greenhouse or skylight windows?

If so, will the extension pole reach, or will you need to rent a boom lift or scissors lift? Skylights or greenhouse windows can be cleaned with an extension pole and a flat squeegee. Otherwise a lift of some kind must be used. Check with the building personnel first to see if the building owners own a lift for the building already; otherwise figure in the cost of renting one. Once the foyer is estimated, check the rest of the building.

How many inside windows on each floor? Are they partition windows between offices or windows that face the exterior?

Count all the windows to be cleaned. Some offices are built with windows facing the hallways or other offices. Some property managers will want these windows cleaned. Be clear as to which windows you are asked to clean.

What size are the windows?

How will the window size effect your pricing? Know your strategy and be consistent.

What type of windows are installed?

Today's office building windows can be very expensive to replace. Certain coatings will scratch with the slightest metal speck caught between squeegee rubber and the window. If you're not experienced with the type of windows used in the building, then ask the property manager or building owner. Ask if the windows have any special tints or laminations.

Do any of the windows have a tint that may be easily scratched?

Maybe the windows have been tinted. Does the tint scratch easily? Look at the windows closely for signs of tint damage. The cheaper the tint, the softer the material needed (like soft cotton) to scrub the glass. Some tints will scratch with the use of a window scrubbing tool.

What covers the office windows?

Each office may be different; maybe the windows have no window coverings; however, if the windows have miniblinds or vertical blinds or other forms of window coverings that must be opened or moved, this takes time.

Opening and closing hundreds of miniblinds or other window coverings can be a day's work by itself. It is virtually guaranteed that a few miniblinds or coverings will stick either in the opening or closing. Plan time for this labor intensive work. It may turn out that opening and closing the window coverings takes more time than the actual window cleaning.

What obstacles are in front of the windows?

When someone occupies an office, they make it their own space. Desks in front of windows can be major time consuming barriers. Potted plants and other possessions in the window sill take time to move. What steps will you take in order to safely clean the windows? Will you ask the office staff to remove window sill items like pictures and collectibles? Or, will you move everything yourself? Imagine a hundred windows with many items to move. Cleaning the actual window might be the easiest part of the window cleaning process.

Is there a special time when the window cleaning will need to be completed?

Some office managers will not want you to work when people are around. They will want the work done either during lunch or at the end of the day or on weekends. What offices need that service? Mark that on the bid sheet. Some offices will refuse any window cleaning or will require you to sign in, wear a security badge, or be escorted. Note these places also on the bid sheet.

When the inspection of the exterior and interior windows is complete, figure out the time needed to complete the non-cleaning tasks.

How much driving time?

If you're paying employees to sit in a car and drive to and from the site, then you may wish to put the driving time into your bid. Maybe use as a rule that every job site over an hour's distance is charged driving time. Use whatever works for you.

How much time to set up the equipment?

If you're setting up and tearing down a water fed pole system with deionization tanks and a few hundred feet of hose, then a set-up and tear-down time charge could be added to the bid.

What equipment will be needed for the job?

Once you have all the information about the building, start to think about what personnel and equipment will be needed.

How many workers?
How many sets of equipment?
Any unusual size squeegees,
handles, or other cleaning
devices needed?
How many extension poles?
How many ladders?
What size ladders?
Will the ladders need ladder levelers?
Will the ladder ends need to be

covered so as not to mark up
or scuff the building wall or
moldings?
What type or types of water keys?
Will you use a water fed system?
Will you need a boom?
Will you need any cones or barrier
        devices to help keep people
        away from   ladders or clean
        ing areas?   Some states have
        laws mandating the use of
cones or other barriers
        marking the use of ladders,
        trucks, and equipment.
What about signs that let   pedestrians
        know of wet walkways?
Will you need extra uniform shirts
        for employees, so that people
        at the building know that you are
        working for the manager or
        building owner?
Building owners and managers appreciate
and sometimes demand the use of a uniformed shirt
that lets them know and the tenants know who
works for the window cleaning company especially
while working inside the buildings and going into
offices.

A few — very few — mid-rise buildings can
only be cleaned from the top down meaning you
need to use a stage or a boatswain's chair, so if all
the other types of equipment will not work, then
think about stages or chairs (more information re-
garding stage and chairwork in the chapter on high-
rise window cleaning.)

Are there any building or safety issues that should be reported to the building owner or manager?

By taking the time to report unsafe areas, you show the building owner or manager that you care about the safety of the people in the building. You also demonstrate your professionalism. What are some of the possible safety issues?

Cracks in the windows

Hardwater stains

Damaged glass

Rubber that holds the window may be
falling out or missing. Sometimes
so many sides of rubber are missing
that the window just sits loosely in
the frame.

Walkways that appear slippery when wet

Broken or errant sprinklers

Tree branches rubbing against the glass

Would the property manager or owner walk the building with you?

It's nice to offer the person asking you to bid if he or she would like to accompany you as you make your initial inspection. This is a chance to begin a working relationship. You're gathering information, listening to the needs of the potential client. Who was the other window cleaning service? What happened to that company? Questions like these probe what was missing from the other window cleaning service. Maybe the other service is doing a lousy job of cleaning. Maybe there was no other service, maybe the owner was rude, maybe they took too long, the potential reasons are endless.

One client told her new window cleaning

company that she came to work one Saturday morning and was working in her office on the 32nd floor when the swing stage with one window cleaner stopped in front of her window. The window cleaner was just a boy no more than 15-years old. Right then and there she knew that she had to find another company for the next window cleaning contract which, at the time, was a $30,000 a year contract.

Another property manager said the other company took two weeks to clean the six office buildings, and she needed the window cleaning completed much quicker and cleaned on the weekends. The new window cleaner completed the window cleaning in two days.

Deliver the bid proposal in a timely manner.

One window cleaner, before his untimely death in a tragic high-rise accident, shared a story about bidding and winning a window cleaning contract. He submitted the bid within one day of surveying the building site. As he cleaned the windows, he noticed a competitor walking up to the building manager and wondering about how the other window cleaner got the job. "He's ready to work," replied the manager, "while you're just getting here with your bid."

Save the information for future reference.

Once you collect all the building information, then you have it for future reference. Save all your data in a notebook or filing system.

When you get the job, you now have all the information on paper and not in your head. You save yourself the grief of trying to remember the building. Look over the building information again, making sure you have all your equipment including water keys. Remind any workers of what to watch out for.

Maybe the job will be cleaned every three months, six months, or yearly. When you get the call that "It's time to clean the windows" then you can look back over your building information sheets to refresh your memory about that building site, what you need and what to look out for. You could even give your workers a copy for review.

Even if you don't get the job, save the bidding information for the future. You never know when that customer will call back and ask you to bid again since most property managers go out to bid once a year on their service contracts.

Now with all the building information, you can prepare the bid.

Chapter 11

BIDDING MID-RISE BUILDINGS

Some window cleaners can just glance at a building and know the bid price; it's a gift. Everyone else needs a sharp pencil and a calculator. Don't leave home without them.

Hopefully, though, along with a pencil and calculator, you create a Bid Information Sheet that has a place to answer all the questions mentioned in the last chapter. Nothing can be more frustrating than missing information about a building before you bid the building or before you clean the windows.

The biggest question, though, is how much do you need to earn for the job to be profitable to you? What is your going rate to make money? The going rate as of the printing of this book was between $50 and $100 per man hour. Working for less money just doesn't pay. How do you figure a bid that equals or exceeds that per hour rate? The best bidding methods include the following:

> by the window,
> by the man hour
> by the day
> by the market pricing

Bidding by the window pane

Counting up the number of windows and the size of these windows and a price per side is a good beginning to the bid process. Having the number of first floor windows and the size of the window, having the number of second story and or third story windows and their sizes gives you solid numbers to work with.

Whether you use those numbers to help calculate the price per window or number of man hours needed to clean the windows, counting windows gives you a concrete number to work with.

The following approximations are not meant to be taken as the absolute final word on pricing per pane, but to be used as a reference point for beginning the bidding process. You will, hopefully, adjust your pricing structure to fit your means.

Office window architecture comes in three different window styles with different pricing structures:

Buildings with exterior walls covered with glass (windows and spandrels).

Buildings with one row of windows on each floor that wraps around the building or most of the building.

Buildings with windows that are grouped together with anywhere from 5 feet to 20 feet of space between each grouping of windows.

This grouping of windows can take many forms:

a row of four or five windows
windows form a large rectangular shape
oversized windows of glass 6 x 6 or larger.

This does not take into account any unusual window placement or greenhouse window designs that will take more time and risk, but just a general window placement.

The following prices offer a place to begin your bidding process. These prices may not be accurate for the time and market in which you are bidding, but they give you an idea.

Sample First Floor

Based on a 4-foot by 6-foot window pane.

1. The entire wall is covered with glass.
   Prices of .75 to $1.50 per pane
2. The windows are all in a row
   wrapping around the building.
   Prices of $1.00 to $2.00 per pane
3. The windows are single or in groups
   of two or three with some distance to
   the next grouping of windows.
   Prices of $2.00 to $3.00 per pane.

Some window cleaners charge a flat rate per window of .75 to $2.00 per pane for first floor windows no matter what the building window formation. Do what works for you.

For second story windows, the prices should be higher although a few window cleaners keep the same price for any first or second floor windows since second story windows means ladders, poles, more difficult cleaning.

Sample Second Floor

Based on a 4-foot by 6-foot window pane

1. The entire wall is covered with glass
   Prices of $1.50 to $2.00 per pane
2. The windows are all in a row wrapping around the building.
   Prices of $2.00 to $3.00 per pane
3. The windows are single or in groups of two or three with some distance to the next grouping of windows.
   Prices of $2.50 to $3.00 per pane.

Bidding by the window pane is usually broken down into a price for the exterior side of the window and a separate price for cleaning the interior of the window.

Interior window cleaning

Building owners may or may not have you clean the windows inside the building. Or, they may ask you to clean them every other time or even once a year.

The cleaning times may vary, so by separating out the bid for interior window cleaning, you and your customer can see the breakdown in pricing. The following example gives you a rough estimate to start bidding interior windows.

Sample Interior
Based on a 4-foot by 6-foot window pane

Interior prices with no ladder work
$1.00 to $2.00 per pane
Interior prices with ladder work
$2.00 to $3.00 per pane

Exterior window cleaning usually is the quickest to clean (no walls, desks, etc.)

Example:
In this example, the building is one where the windows wrap around all four sides of the building. Each side looks exactly the same. Each window is 4-foot by 6-foot. The owner wants a bid for one time only. For the sake of simplicity and approximation, the amount of $2.00 per window on the first floor and $3.00 a window on the second floor will be used for windows which are 4-foot by 6-foot. What you actually charge will vary according to the exterior window formations and the size of the windows, but for simplicity, the windows are flush against the wall and the wall texture is rough, sandblasted concrete.

Example A

First floor: 20 windows per side x 4 sides
second floor: 20 windows per side x 4 sides
The building has four doors.

Total
First floor = 80 windows
Second floor = 80 windows
four doors (in & out) = 8 windows

How much would you bid?

First floor windows	$2 x 80	=	$160
Second floor windows	$3 x 80	=	$240
Four doors	$2 x 8	=	$ 16
	Total	=	$416

Now, if this price is below your minimum, then you charge the minimum price. After cleaning these windows, are you going to go out and clean another building? Probably not. So, what is your minimum charge?

By the hour

Bidding by the hour means estimating how long it will take you to clean the windows. Some window cleaners look at the job and can estimate roughly a day's work instead of how many hours. But still, breaking the time down by sections of a building and adding these totals also gives them another method for estimating a job.

172

For instance look at the last example. If the building is bid by the hour it may look something like example B.

Example B

First floor: 20 windows per side x 4 sides
second floor: 20 windows per side x 4 sides
The building has four doors.

First floor = 20 windows per side = 1/2 hour
Second floor = 20 windows per side = 1/2 hour
four doors (in & out) = 8 windows 2mins/window

First floor = four sides x 1/2 hour per side = 2 hours
Second floor = four sides x 1/2 hour per side = 2 hours
four doors @ 2 minutes per door   = 10 minutes
Set up time   = 10 minutes
tear down time   = 10 minutes

Driving time? (add if necessary)

Total	=	4 1/2 hours
Hourly rate	=	$100 / hour
$100 x 4 1/2 hours	=	$450.00
Bid price	=	$450.00

Bidding by the hour works well with unusual window designs where the windows are placed in a grouping of windows, Figure 1, or extra large plates of glass like a 10-foot by 10-foot window pane with a large half-circle window above it. Maybe the windows are not standard size or maybe they are an unusual combination of glass with sections and unusual challenges to get to them. Then bidding by the hour becomes the bidding tool. As an example look at the windows in figure 1. First, just picture each grouping of windows. Imagine you're walking up to the window set. Imagine you're cleaning the windows at a safe professional speed.

How long did it take you to clean that set of windows?

Now, multiply that time by the number of sets of windows like that on the building, add time for driving, setting up, and tearing down. Now take that number and multiply it by how much you wish to earn an hour and you have yourself a bid price.

How long it takes to clean each window will vary depending on the quality of the cleaning you want to perform.

For first floor windows, the time needed for cleaning can be anywhere from one minute to three minutes per 4-foot by 6-foot window without the need for an extension pole.

Extension pole work can be up to five minutes a window depending on the size. If you're just going to clean the windows with no attention to the moldings, then the cleaning will go faster. If you wipe down the moldings with careful detail, then the cleaning time will be longer.

What type of job do you want to perform?

Are you going to set yourself up as a quality window cleaning service or one that will be keenly competitive, getting the window cleaning completed in the fastest time possible?

Figure 1:

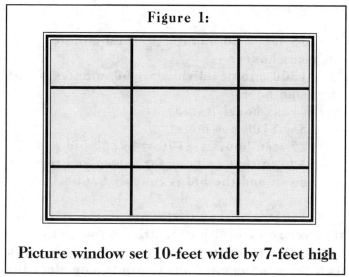

Picture window set 10-feet wide by 7-feet high

Take for example a building with window sets that look like the one in Figure 1. The building has 75 sets of windows that look like this set.

Imagine how long these windows would take to clean on the exterior. These windows may take anywhere from 10 to 20 minutes per set of windows if you include all the cleaning activities: cleaning, walking between sets, wiping frames, etc. Many window cleaners will speed through the window cleaning and, quite frankly, clean the windows faster. The point, though, is to clean the windows at a relaxed, not break neck, speed. And, in this case, also include the time for moving to and from window sets and other time wasters: going back to the truck, getting more water, taking a few breaks to restore your energy, etc.

If you say the time necessary is 20 minutes to clean all the windows and moldings, then multiply that time by the 75 sets of windows used in the example.

75 sets x 20 minutes = 1500 minutes

How many hours?

1500 minutes divided by 60 minutes = 25 man hours

What is your hourly rate?

Say $100 per hour

25 man hours x $100 = $2500 bid price

Add to that an hour for set-up and tear-down and the bid is roughly $2600.

You can discount the job if you wish, but this gives you an initial bid price. Too many window cleaners underestimate the time needed to clean the windows and then rush to complete the job. They get fooled by the size of the task. By breaking down the window cleaning into smaller sections and then multiplying that by the number of sections, you get a more accurate picture of the hours needed to complete the task.

Can the job be cleaned at a faster rate? Absolutely, but you want to bid the job giving the maximum amount of time it may take to clean the windows and moldings and cover all the other in between time wasters.

Bidding by the day

Some window cleaning companies bid the job by the day. That is they know that the job will take approximately one day or less to complete, and they bid the job by how much they want to earn in a day per man. Larger companies pay a per diem rate for workers. When the job finishes in less than a day and there isn't enough time to go out on another job, they will, most likely, bid their daily rate and not a per hour rate. They still want to earn a day's wage. Smaller companies can get away with working by the hourly rate. Larger companies with full-time employees cannot. They need to bid as if the job would take the entire workday.

With experience, a window cleaner can glance at a building and know the building will take roughly a day to clean, and then they bid their daily rate.

Market Price Approach

Free enterprise is alive and well in the window cleaning business. Your competitors set the tone for the pricing structure for some buildings. A property manager may not be able to change the current window cleaning price more than a five percent varience from last year's window cleaning contract. He or she may just tell you that the budget for the window cleaning for a particular building is "X" dollars and that the price can not go above that amount.

Maybe your bid is significantly different from the other competitors and the property manager wants to know the reason. If you feel strongly that your price is a fair price, then explain your price with conviction. If you really want the job, then consider discounting your price, but know your limit and don't be afraid to walk away from the job.

Minimum charge

There is the question of a minimum charge. How much is the least amount for which you are willing to go out and clean the windows? For office buildings, most window cleaners look at their daily rate and use that as their minimum. After you clean one small office building that takes maybe four hours, you're not going to go out to another building. You'll be tired from the first job. Many window cleaners use a dollar figure that equals close to what they wish to earn daily.

Professionalism pays in the long run.

Don't be afraid to ask for your price. Once you set the tone for your company's image, one of the highest professionalism, then customers are more likely to accept your pricing structure. Remember, you're not cleaning the windows at record speed. You're cleaning the windows at a safe and professional speed. By accurately judging how long the job will take, you give yourself and your employees enough time for safe and professional results. Will another window cleaning service come in at a cheaper price? Possibly, but at what cost are you going to lower your price? Faster window cleaning? Cutting corners with the service? Paying your labor "under the table"? Not paying taxes, not using the best equipment?

The safety, integrity and structure of your business is most important.

Chapter 12

BIDDING HIGH-RISE

Please note: Before attempting to clean high-rise windows, a window cleaner needs to be properly trained in the use of the equipment. Please take the time to learn the equipment, learn the job hazards, and learn the safety precautions. Hazards abound in high-rise work. Contact the International Window Cleaning Association for more information about high-rise window cleaning work and safety.

The following chapter is a brief look at bidding methods for high-rise window cleaning. Written for the American Window Cleaner magazine, the leading window cleaning magazine, this chapter is not a comprehensive examination of the subject. It is also not meant to fuel the fires of the scaffolding versus the "descent control device" controversy. Its main purpose is to inform window cleaners how high-rise window cleaning companies bid in a simple form, what they look for and what they earn. The bidding methods are for window cleaners that use a boatswain's chair or scaffolding.

More than any other type of window cleaning, high-rise window cleaning and bidding can make even the most youthful of window cleaners prematurely gray. The information needed to insure an effective bid proposal is great. Gathering pertinent information and staying competitive but profitable in your bidding helps keep companies not only competitive but financially successful.

Getting the important building information

The following information was gathered by interviewing six prominent window cleaners from around the country. Most of them commented that high-rise bidding takes experience.

Before the bidding, though, each of these window cleaners spent a good deal of time gathering some or all of the following information about a building.

What is the Traveling Time to the Job Site?

Unlike most house or storefront window cleaners, many high-rise companies travel, sometimes great distances, to accommodate good customers. At some point, there may be a need to figure in the cost of traveling to and from the job. What if the building is an hour's drive or more? This may need to be figured into the labor needed for the job. As one window cleaner said, "We have jobs that require two hours of driving to the job and two hours back from the job leaving four working hours at the job site."

What does the roof look like?

Here begins the process of "laying" out the job, deciding equipment needed, how to rig it and how to get the equipment up to the roof.

Is the roof level?

Are there obstacles to work around like air conditioners? Obstacles will eat time in setting up the rigging and re-rigging.

What additional equipment will be needed on the roof?

Some property managers will not allow you to walk on the roof without laying down 4-foot by 8-foot sheets of plywood.

How high is the parapet wall? Can it accept any weight?

If a window cleaning company works with "controlled descent devices" and, maybe, "rolling roof rigs" then information about the parapet wall can be crucial and beyond the scope of this book. How well constructed is the parapet wall? Some parapets consist of a material call "Dryvitt" that is almost like styrofoam and can accept no weight.

Does the building have its own scaffolding?

If the building does have scaffolding, when was the last time the equipment was inspected? Does it receive regular maintenance? You may demonstrate a high degree of professionalism with your own equipment: regular maintenance, removing all worn ropes or mechanical equipment, replacing them with the highest quality for safety reasons, but your customer may not. Will you ask to see the equipment maintenance records?

If the customer does not have scaffolding but does have the davits and tie backs, the window cleaner needs to use his own scaffolding or rent the equipment. The cost of scaffolding rental can be over $400 per day. Then, it needs to be transported to the job site and the roof.

Some companies own their own scaffolding and don't charge for its use but do charge a transportation and set-up fee of up to $400.

Many newer buildings now come equipped with their own scaffolding that will usually save the window cleaner and building owner the added expense of scaffolding.

Does the building have davits and tie backs?

If the building doesn't have its own scaffolding, then you need to find out if the building has the davits and tie backs from which to hang the scaffolding. If not, an outrigger system may be necessary to complete the window cleaning. An outrigger system uses a series of counterweights to hold the rigging in place.

Extra time should mean extra money. Some companies charge up to $800 per job to supply an outrigger while others charge less.

If you use scaffolding, what size stage will the davits hold?

The distance between davits determines the size of the scaffolding. This information determines the number of "drops" necessary to clean the building. Shorter scaffolding means more "drops" and more changing over time.

What electrical outlets are available?

On occasion, special adaptations are necessary to allow the window cleaner's equipment to operate. There is sometimes a need to match the electrical plug and outlet, so the equipment can operate properly.

How accessible is the roof?

Sometimes getting equipment or a window cleaner to the roof poses a problem. Usually the elevator does not go to the roof which means lugging equipment upstairs, sometimes two floors.

After a roof inspection you figure the number of "drops," whether by stage or chair, to clean the windows. Determining the number or "drops" is a crucial part of the formula in bidding a building's window cleaning.

Is the building glass and spandrels (curtain wall glass) or glass and concrete?

Buildings that are all glass take longer to clean which will effect how many "drops" you can achieve in a day.

How long will it take to set up on the roof?

Once you have the roof information, you can judge how long the initial rigging time will take. Again, experience is the best teacher. It could take two window cleaners an hour to two and a half hours to set-up rigging. If the roof access is difficult and equipment has to be lugged up flights of stairs, the set-up time increases. For instance, one window cleaner lamented that it took a crew of five big guys to carry a 1400 pound stage up flights of stairs. When they finally had the stage set up and ready for window cleaning, half the day was gone. The lesson learned: Be realistic about the moving of equipment and set-up time.

How many floors to the building or what is the building height?

Knowing the number of floors to the building or height of the building helps determine roughly how long it will take to drop down the side of a building. How many drops, or how many times window cleaners must descend down the side of the building depends on the building's size and the equipment used.

If you use controlled descent devices (boatswain's chairs) then the maximum lateral distance you can safely clean windows would be six feet to either side of the chair (as recommended in the IWCA safety guidelines. For more information call the IWCA at 1-800-875-4922).

If scaffolding is used, then the size of the scaffolding becomes the lateral distance you can safely clean the glass. Scaffolding (swing stages) come in sizes from 16' to 32' lengths. And the stage sizes that can be used will be determined by the distance between the davits.

Labor Time on a Building

In a recent poll, high-rise window cleaners were asked for rough estimates of the time it takes to descend different size buildings. These estimates were based on a "good" day with no complications in the "drop" or "changeover" or time.

The following times were estimated by surveying window cleaners that use a 28-foot scaffolding.

Sample Times
All Glass Building
10-story building   (2 1/2 - 3 hours per drop)
20 story building   (5 - 6 hours per drop)
40 story building   (6 - 7 hours per drop)

Glass and Concrete Building
10-story building   1/2 to 1 1/2 hours per drop
20-story building   1 to 2-hours per drop
40-story building   3 to 4-hours per drop

Note: The higher the building the more wind becomes a problem hampering the window cleaning. Also, extra time may be needed to refill buckets.

Some states have height restrictions on controlled descent devices. (i.e. California's Cal-OSHA does not allow the use of these devices on buildings over 130 feet). It's important to check

local regulations. Also, recent guidelines by the
ANSI A-39 committee, recommended that rolling
roof rigs not operate in a lateral motion with a
worker in the chair. So, these boatswain's chair
"drops" are down only.

The Formula

Once all this information is gathered, the
time needed to complete the job is calculated.

Drive time x # of workers (if needed)=

___ labor hours

Set-up time x # of workers=

___ labor hours

Drop time x # of workers x # of drops =

___ labor hours

Changeover time x # of workers x #of drops   =

___ labor hours

Tear down time x # of workers =

___ labor hours

Total labor hours =

___ labor hours

Some companies round off the labor hours
to a day's work since many employees are paid by
the day. They still get paid a full day's work even
though they finish the job early on the last day, so
when bidding the jobs, consider rounding the bid
out to a day's work even though it may be short of
a day's work.

Total labor x hourly rate $_____   Subtotal
Equipment rental charges $_____
Total Initial bid   = $_____

What should a company charge per hour?

What you charge for work is your business; however, the better the hourly rate the better the cash flow.

As of this writing, the average hourly rate for high-rise window cleaning was between $50 and $100 per hour. Sometimes, though, the hourly rate for high-rise window cleaning is less than other types of window cleaning. As one window cleaner lamented, "I make as much per hour cleaning storefront windows with less worry." There are window cleaners that can boast of $100 or $200 per hour for "gravy" jobs. However, there are also those window cleaners with a woeful tale of the nightmare job that ends up costing them money. Yes, it is important to get the job, but it is more important to make money with the highest degree of safety.

Labor Costs

The costs of labor or what companies pay their employees varies considerably. As a percentage, the employee costs averaged between 25 percent and 45 percent of what the company billed per hourly rate. These percentages did not include workers' compensation costs that, in some states, can run as high as 100 percent of your labor costs. Which means, if a company pays a window cleaner $12.00 per hour, then the workers' compensation is also $12 per hour. After paying social security and other incidentals (truck and equipment depreciation, insurance, etc.) the costs add up.

Contract Labor

A few companies interviewed wanted to comment on the growing use of contract labor. Contract labor, sometimes known as piece work, is paying a worker as an independent contractor and offering a percentage of the job upon completion of the work. By knowing what percentage of the bid will be used for labor, window cleaners can guarantee the profit they want from the job. For instance, if a job will pay $100 and you offer a window cleaner, 40 percent of what the job will pay, then he earns $40. That's piece work.

The contracted laborer knows what the job will pay and may be motivitated to work harder. If the worker finishes the job sooner, they still receive the same pay. In his type of working arrangement, many contracted window cleaners rush the job to earn more money per hour for the job.

It's the rushing to finish that gets the window cleaners in trouble. As Stefan Bright, Safety Director with the International Window Cleaning Association says, "The 'hurry up syndrome' is when 99.9% of all window cleaning accidents occur."

It's the belief of some interviewees that this practice of using contract labor leads to accidents and even fatalities when workers are subjected to such motivations. Window cleaning companies are encouraged to hire workers as employees. This "Hurry up syndrome" can have a devastating effect on business.

With building owners and managers, the higher the quality of work you deliver to your customers, the greater your chances of earning a higher hourly rate. Many building managers and owners demand quality window cleaning work, and they will, in the long run, recognize quality and, in many cases, pay more for that service.

Let the customer know that your price represents the highest quality service using the safest cleaning methods available. For many window cleaning companies, this philosophy has helped them grow not only reputable but highly profitable businesses as well.

Marketing approach to bidding

Finding out what building owners, property managers, or janitorial companies are paying for work gives you a general sense of what people are paying for window cleaning in that area. Sometimes they will tell you, sometimes they won't.

When it comes to bidding a job, it doesn't hurt to ask what the job price was last year or the last time the building was cleaned. Again, sometimes they'll tell you, sometimes they won't.

Getting a sense of the past pricing helps in a number of ways. Sometimes a building's window cleaning can be complex: the cleaning may require stage work, chair work, a boom, and extension ladders— in other words, a bidding nightmare.

Asking the owner or manager what price they have in mind tells you what that person or company is accustomed to paying and gives you a realistic idea of where the property manager or owner feels the price should be.

Also, many property managers have a ceiling price on what they can pay above last year's price for window cleaning. Even though they are searching for another window cleaner, they usually wish to stay within 5% of last year's window cleaning budget. Maybe the old window cleaner's price was too cheap and the window cleaning was rushed and sloppy. Then you have to convince the property manager or owner why the higher price is justified.

Finally, by using the marketing approach to bidding, you gather data on what other window cleaners charge and can gather valuable pricing information about your competition giving you some idea how you compare to the competition. The information can help you differentiate your company from the others.

The rushed job is an accident waiting to happen. Be sure you bid high enough that you can earn what you're worth and not attempt to cut corners or rush the job just to earn a higher hourly rate. Take the time to set up the job safely.

Take the time to check and recheck equipment.

Rushing a window cleaning job may earn you a few extra bucks per hour, but someone getting hurt or killed on your job will plague you the rest of your natural life.

Think about it.

Chapter 8

POST CONSTRUCTION CLEANUPS

After the construction of a house, a storefront or office building completed, one of the final jobs to be done is what's called Post Construction Cleanup. In general, the term means the final cleanup before the homeowner or business person moves in.

These jobs can look like easy money, but don't let them fool you. Post Construction Cleanups can be your worst nightmare for a couple of reasons.

First, the chances of scratching glass and causing significant damage to windows is greatest in construction cleanup jobs. Those fine scratch lines that your scraper "may" leave on the glass are hard to see in the shade or cloudy days, but they become much more obvious when the sun filters through the window, and you're asked to replace the windows.

Second, a Post Construction Cleanup can take much longer to clean than what you thought. The objects and material stuck to the glass and moldings may not want to come off the way you figured they would, and Murphy's Law, "Whatever you plan will usually take longer and cost more," will come into play on construction cleanups.

If you should decide to bid these jobs, here are a few tips to help you.

Ten Tips to Better Post Construction Cleanup

This is by no means a complete handbook on post construction cleanup jobs, but these ten tips would be a start in the right direction.

1. Close inspection of glass for scratches and imperfections before beginning a job and informing the supervisors or owners of the scratches will save you from getting blamed for them later.

2. Scratches found during the cleaning should halt the work and be brought to the supervisors' or owners' attention before resuming the job.

3. House glass is much softer than industrial glass and is more susceptible to scratching; therefore, more care and concern should be taken in its cleaning.

4. Overcast skies, nighttime, and shade tend to hide or mask any scratches that may be occuring. Working on glass with at least some sunlight shows all the imperfections in glass including any scratches.
5. Frequent changing of worn razor blades helps

prevent scratching. (This one is tough because no one wants to stop when they have a rhythm going.) However, reinforcing a habit of changing blades will help insure that you are using clean sharp blades.

Change razor blades immediately when the blade gets a chip or crack. It may not look as though that razor is causing a problem on the glass, but as you work the blade is getting worse and will start causing problems.

6. Test a small area of glass first with a razor blade or scrub pads to see how it reacts to cleaning with a razor. Some windows will not tolerate a razor on the glass and you can tell immediately, and only certain scrub pads can be used on the glass.

7. Scrape the window in a forward direction and then lift the blade off the glass when pulling it backward. Sliding the razor backward while it's still on the glass can cause a tiny rock or piece of stucco to be caught between the blade and the glass which can cause it to scratch.

8. Scrape only the areas of glass that need it. Scraping the entire window when it only has a few paint marks is an unnecessary risk.

9. Move cautiously, carefully, and slowly when using a razor blade. Nothing causes more accidents or damaged glass more than moving too quickly. Your body can get ahead of your thinking process and you may do some damage to the glass or cause an accident.

10. Spend extra time training yourself and employees on the proper and safe usage of a razor blade. Don't assume employees know the proper usage. Test them.

Bidding Post Construction Cleanups

What material will need to be scraped from the glass? Each Post Construction Cleanup site has a personality all its own and can be considered in terms of various degrees of amount of work needed to be done.

The question is what percentage of the window will need to be scraped? Some Post Construction Cleanups have less than ten percent of the window needing to be scraped or scrubbed while some P.C.C.'s will have all the windows 100 percent covered with paint, cement, and silicon. Then there are the various levels of PCC cleaning in between.

The other question to be answered is what is the material to be scraped? Some materials like plaster can come off easily with soap, water, and a little scrubbing. Other materials like silicon can be a time consuming chore of scraping and rubbing. (Some powder acids do remove silicon from the glass, but they are not the easiest materials to use.) In general, window cleaners bid between two to six times the regular window cleaning price for those same windows.

Like bidding other types of window cleaning, houses, storefronts, or small office buildings, P.C.C.'s involve some of the same questions about the job, plus a few more. Review the chapters about bidding those types of windows first before continuing with this chapter.

Basically, bidding P.C.C.'s is the same as bidding the regular window cleaning price but then you multiply that figure by a number between two and six depending on the amount of work involved for each window.

These multiples between two and six are based upon the degree of material (stucco, paint, silicone, rubber buttons, or plaster) left on the glass. Here is where experience becomes the best teacher. After a while you can look at a P.C.C. and get a feel for how much work each window will take. When judging the percentage of window surface area to be scraped, some windows will be covered with material to be scraped while other windows will be almost clean of material to be scraped, so take an average.

You can do this by laying out columns on a blank, white paper and noting the different windows and percentage of scraping work needed or you can just make a mental note as you walk the job counting windows.

The following five sections offer a rough sample of potential ways of using the multiple.

No multiple necessary

Some P.C.C.'s need little or no extra work and, therefore, only the regular window cleaning price is charged. Usually the paint spray is minimal, a few spots. The moldings are basically clean except for a few spots of paint or plaster. In this case you may not wish to change your basic window cleaning price, or you may wish to pad the bid some just in case the cleaning takes longer than expected. A ten to twenty percent increase from the regular window cleaning price is reasonable.

Multiply the regular window cleaning price by two

Each window contains some extra cleaning where the window may need to be washed and squeegeed at least twice. The amount of material to scrape or clean off the glass is **25** percent or less, and when you wet the window once, clean the material off the glass and moldings and then squeegee, you would probably notice that you left some window area that may need to be cleaned again. So, you have to rewet the glass and remove that remaining material; thus a reason for doubling the regular window cleaning price.

Multiply the regular window cleaning price by three, four, or five

Here is where the bidding gets tricky. Judging how much window area must be scraped or scrubbed or how difficult the material will be to remove becomes a judgment. The more P.C.C.'s you clean the better you get at judging the job.

Here are a few possible reasons for using higher multiples. These are not hard and fast rules for bidding P.C.C.'s, but a gauge to start the bidding process. After you complete a few jobs, then adjust this information to fit your own window cleaning needs.

Multiple of three times the regular window cleaning price

The average window area is covered **50** per-

196

cent or less and the moldings are not that spotted and easy to clean.

Maybe the window is clean except for the rubber "buttons" cover the glass on one or both sides. Those little black rubber buttons are used to separate the glass plates during transportation and take time to remove. They tend to leave little gum residues that must be removed either by scraping or rubbing and there are usually enough of them to slow the job down.
When there are just a few of the little "buggers" on the glass, that's not too bad; however, when the window is covered, then the cleaning can become tedious and slow, much more than you might expect.

The moldings are covered with paint, plaster and cement, but the windows have little material on them.

Sometimes you don't need to spend extra time cleaning the window but extra time cleaning the moldings. Some job supervisors or janitorial companies (if you're contracted by a janitorial company) spend more time inspecting the moldings than the windows. Moldings can take more time to clean than the window cleaning. Concrete will stain certain moldings if it is not cleaned off within a short time period.

Multiple of four to six times the window cleaning price.

The majority of windows and moldings are covered with material that needs to be scraped. Here the mulitple used will depend on the degree of difficulty and how many times you'll need to go over the window (usually twice). Then you need

to take into account the moldings which can actually take more time to clean than the windows. If
the material is plaster, that usually comes off with
soap and water and maybe a little scraping. If the
material is paint overspray, concrete, or silicon,
than scraping and scrubbing is necessary.
You make the decision.

Adjusting your price
Each window cleaner will have a different
view of what the job will take.
Besides the window cleaner's view and ability, each job will vary. Maybe the percentage of
material on the glass is not that much, but the type
of material to remove is much tougher than normal (type of paint or stucco, etc.)— then adjust
the price to the next higher multiple. Or, maybe
the percentage of material to be removed covers
the glass but requires little effort and is much
easier to remove (some wall plaster comes off with
just wetting the window with the scrubber)—then
you can adjust the multiple down.
The above multiples for pricing are just a
starting point to use as you wish. Each window
cleaning company will have a different view of what
will be needed to earn money on a P.C.C. job.
What one company can accomplish in a certain
time period, another window cleaner may take
twice as long, maybe producing a higher quality of
work.
Remember, though, the faster you go, the
greater chance of an accident.
Safety first.

When the Job Superintendent dislikes the bid

When you meet with the job superinten-
dent and he tells you that your bid is way too high,
you might check your figures again, or you might
just walk away. These P.C.C.'s are generally not
regular jobs. They're here and gone, and the risk
taken in cleaning these jobs can be far greater than
the regular window cleaning jobs.

Regular service jobs are what helps keep a
window cleaning business stable. Unless you're
really hungry for the work or you have the extra
manpower to complete the job, stand by your
price.

Explain to the job superintendent why the
price is the way it is, justify your price and that
you're worth the money.

The object is to make money.

Those window cleaners that try to bid com-
petitively and then find themselves hurrying
through the job because the cleaning is taking
longer to complete than they thought are setting
themselves up for costly mistakes: scratched glass
or injured workers.

Afterword

The first meeting of the International Window Cleaning Association

Top row: Jim Willingham, Sorbo Samuelsson, David Barnes   Second row: Jon Capon, James Gilmore, Steven Miller, Jackie Kopp, Carl Pedersen, Brad Martin, Herb Herzel, John Baxter First row: Richard Fabry, Stan Ehrenkranz, Jeffery Valcourt & Friend, Vickie Wagner, Charles Dedden Seated:Michael Smahlik, Marty Racenstein

202

I REMEMBER LUBBOCK

A DEDICATION TO THE MEN AND WOMEN OF THE IWCA

Not long ago, a small group of men and women held a meeting in the suite of a Lubbock, Texas hotel. Their goal was to begin a window cleaning association that would help unite and serve the window cleaning industry long fragmented with strife and disunity. This group of men and women made up of window cleaning companies from around the United States and Canada, had come to the first window cleaning convention and speed window cleaning contest ever held in the United States.

From the first day of the convention, attendees discussed the needs of the industry and wanted to learn more about enhancing professionalism in their own businesses. Throughout the seminars and trade show, many of the window cleaners murmured the same thought: The convention was a wonderful experience; we should do this more often; and there should be some type of window cleaning organization. Some attendees stood-up at seminars and openly suggested, "We need a window cleaning organization."

That night in the suite of Mike Smalik, former president of Ettore products, and with the help of Marty Racenstein, co-owner of J. Racenstein & Company, the first meeting of what was to become known as the International Window Cleaning Association began.

There was an atmosphere that something great was about to happen in that room; that the window cleaning industry would never be the same after that night. The unity, the cooperation, and the compassion these people felt to the effort was electrifying.

At first the vision was for a national organization but as the conversation ensued, a vision of an international association developed and thus opened the doors for a global organization that welcomed window cleaners from around the world.

A president was chosen to head the organization— Jackie Kopp, a woman with vast experience with organizations and who knew how to develop a process for the IWCA's creation. A board of directors was picked from the group.
Suddenly, the IWCA became a reality , and the emotion and exhilaration will not be forgotten by those who were there at that first meeting. You can hear many of the old timers still say today, "I remember Lubbock."

Over the years, these men and women have given their time and money — lots of money — to

204

a belief in unifying their profession, to create for the present and future window cleaners a place, an ideal, and a model for new window cleaners to learn a professional way of creating a window cleaning business.

In the days that followed that fateful day in Lubbock, disagreements arose, feelings were ruffled, after all window cleaners are an independent bunch. After a while, though, people would begin to loosen their independent will and look to the mission statement of the IWCA. Only by working as team players and learning to compromise and unify did the IWCA grow and prosper to the organization it is today and will be for future generations.

The founding members have long since stepped aside, but new members carry on the work of the association with just as much dedication and commitment.

Window cleaners with ambitions and goals of developing the most professional window cleaning business can find the best information, help, and insight through joining the IWCA organization.

Nowhere else will you find a group of more dedicated, responsible, and professional men and women ready and willing to assist and challenge window cleaners to the highest professionalism possible.

Join today.

APPENDIX

SUMMARY OF QUESTIONS

The following is the list of questions from each chapter. Use this section as an easy reference.

"+" = means more time needed for the cleaning
"—" means less time needed for cleaning

HOUSE WINDOW CLEANING
Driving Time?
How far are you willing to travel before you charge for travel time?

The Layout of the home
+   Large home with a few windows per room (more time per window)
—   Large home with many windows per room (less time per window)
How much distance between the windows?
+   The longer the distance, the more time needed
—   The shorter the distance the less time needed

More windows per room means quicker cleaning time per window.

Are the windows reachable without a ladder?

+   Ladders take time to set up and climb plus raise the risk of cleaning windows.

—   No ladder needed means less time for setting up between windows.

Will a ladder be needed for the outside?

+   Setting up, moving, climbing, and taking down a ladder adds time to the cleaning process.

How many times will the ladder be moved?

+   The more times you need to set up the more time added for cleaning.

Will a ladder be needed for the inside?

+   Inside ladder work takes more time.

Can the second floor windows be removed and cleaned from the inside?

—   On sliding windows, the slider pops out of the track allowing the window cleaner to clean the window from the inside.

What type and size are the windows?

+   The larger the windows the more time needed

+   French windows take time to clean

Are the screens new or old?

+   Old screens weathered and rusted will take longer to remove.

—   New screens usually pop up effortlessly.

Are the screens fastened to the window frame?

+   Sometimes homeowners screw the screen to the window.

Are the screens security screens?

+   That little plug to the window can cause all sorts of problems.

Do the screens remove from the inside or the outside?

+ Screens removed from the inside take more time (twice as much time).

— Screens removed from the outside take less time.

How much dirt build up on the outside?

— Less dust and dirt means faster cleaning.

+ More dirt and mud means cleaning some windows twice to remove all the dirt plus changing bucket water more often.

Do the windows have any paint spots or overspray?

+ Add time for scraping (possible extra charge)

Any tape, stickers, or other decorations on the windows?

+ Add time if owner wants the items removed.

Do the windows have any hard water spots?

+ Hard water stain removal can take the window cleaning up to five times longer per window. If you provide this service, charge more.

Any smoke or heavy dirt build up on the inside?

+ Smoke and dirt build up means cleaning some windows twice.

Are the windows tinted?

+ Extra care is needed with tinted glass.

Does the owner want the window tracks cleaned?

+ Some owners want the window tracks perfect. A flat screwdriver usually does the job, but the job takes time.

What is the layout of the ground around the house?

+ Obstacles (fences, plants, etc) add time.

— Unobstructed, level ground quickens the cleaning.

What obstacles lay in the way of the window cleaners inside the house?

+ Furniture, window coverings, etc, blocking the windows can make the cleaning twice as long.

Will the homeowner move some items away from the windows?

Will extra care be needed inside the home?
What type of homeowner personality are you dealing with?

STOREFRONTS
The following is a list of questions that storefront window cleaners should think about while bidding storefront windows.
What is the travel time to the job?
Will you pickup other stores in the same center or same area? Or, is this job the only one?
How many windows to clean?
How often will the windows be cleaned outside?
How often will the inside be cleaned?
Are there many signs to remove from the window or can you work around them?
Are there tables or merchandise to be moved before cleaning the inside?
How often are the outside windows to be cleaned?
How often are the inside windows to be cleaned?
Who are the competitors?
What is the going hourly rate for the area?

MID-RISE BUILDINGS
The following is a list of important questions that mid-rise window cleaners should know before bidding or cleaning the windows of a mid-rise building.
Create a bid sheet with these questions so anytime you bid a building, these questions are handy and you can just fill in the blanks with the answers. Keep as a reference even if you do not get the job.

Outside the building
What is the traveling time to the site?
Who is the contact for the building?
What is the phone number, address, and simple direc-

tions to the building?

Are there any brochures, pamphlets, or copies of the building or business park layout?

What service is required and how often?

Besides clean windows, what are the concerns of the building manager or owner?

What is the layout of the building?

Where is the water outlet?

What type of water key is needed?

What are the sizes and shapes of the windows?

Do the windows open?

Does the building have just windows or is the entire building covered with glass?

How many windows on each floor?

What is the composition of the building exterior?

Are there any cracks, scratches, stains, or damaged windows?

Are the stains on the glass? Calcium deposits? Hardwater stains? Lime stains?

Are the windows flush with the wall or are they set in from the wall?

If the windows are set in from the wall, how far in?

What does the ground and landscape look like?

Are there any obstacles?

Trees against windows?

Cars in the way?

How high up the wall are the windows?

How would you describe the ground around the building?

> Planted?
> Cement?
> Grass?
> Combination of things?

What other obstacles are in the way?

Powerlines?

Heavy foot traffic areas?
Walls, fences, locked gates? window canopies, air
conditioning units? other obstacles?
Which way does the sun cross the sky in relationship
to the buildings?
What unusual window placements or building designs
make cleaning more difficult?

Inside the building
What about the inside window cleaning?
Is there an inside foyer two stories or higher?
Will stairs obstruct the window cleaning?
Any greenhouse or skylight windows?
How many windows on each floor?
Do the windows not facing the exterior need cleaning
also (partition glass)? How many windows?
What is the size of the windows?
What type of window is installed?
Do any of the windows have a tint or coating that may
be easily scratched?
What type of window coverings are used? Miniblinds?
What obstructions are in front of the windows?
Is there any special time when the window cleaning
will need to be done inside or outside? nights?
lunchtime? weekends?
How much time is needed to set up the equipment?
What equipment will be needed for the job?
    How many sets of equipment?
    Any unusual size squeegees or other window
cleaning devices?
    How many extension poles?
    How many ladders?
    What size ladders?
    Will the ladders need ladder levelers?
    Will the ladder ends need to be covered so as
not to mark the building wall or moldings?
    What type or types of water keys needed?

If a waterfed pole system is used, how many waterfed poles will be used? How many feet of hose is needed? How many hoses?

Will you need deionized water tanks?

Pliers? screwdrivers? replacement parts?

Cones, barriers or signs?

How many workers will be needed?

Are there any building or safety issues that should be reported to the building owner or manager?

HIGH-RISE

Note:

Many of the mid-rise questions would also fit in the high-rise category. For sake of simplicity, only the questions related to high-rise window cleaning are placed here.

This is not a comprehensive list for high-rise window cleaning and companies wanting to go into the high-rise window cleaning business should seek out expert help. Contact the International Window Cleaning Association for more information at 1-800-875-4922 or at www.iwca.org

What is the traveling time to the job site?

What does the roof look like?

Is the roof level?

What additional equipment will be needed on the roof?

What about the parapet wall?

How high is the parapet wall?

Can the parapet wall accept weight?

Does the building have its own scaffolding?

Does the building have davits and tie backs?

If scaffolding is needed, what size stage will the davits hold?

What electrical outlets are available?

How accessible is the roof?
Is the building exterior glass and spandrels or glass and concrete?
How much time will be needed to set up the equipment on the roof?
How many floors to the building?
What is the building height?

Index

INDEX

INDEX

INDEX

INDEX

If you are serious about becoming the most professional window cleaning company possible, then join the International Window Cleaning Association.

The IWCA was created to give you a place to learn how to become the best window cleaning company. In the IWCA you will find hundreds of highly successful men and women that know what it takes to grow a successful business; they have experienced the growing pains of the beginning, growing and maturing stages of the window cleaning business.

If you have questions...
the IWCA has answers.

Call them today.

IWCA

International Window Cleaning Association

1-800-875-4922

Visit their website at ww.iwca.org

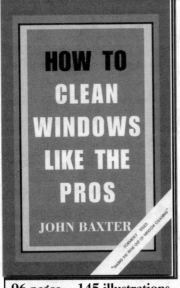
224